AlphaforStudents

First published 2000

New edition 2002

Published by Alpha International, Holy Trinity Brompton, Brompton Road, London SW7 1JA

Printed in the UK by TPS Print, 5 Tunnel Avenue, Greenwich, London SE10 0SL

Telephone: 020 8269 1222. Layout by *Truth* 07900 560 516

Contents

Introduction

Welcome to *The A-Z of Running Alpha for Students*. Its aim is to help, equip and support you whether you know nothing about Alpha for Students or have been running the course for many years. We want you to feel prepared to reach out to your university or college in a way that is both effective and culturally relevant. The manual is intended mainly to help courses in the United Kingdom, although it should also prove relevant for those of you who are planning courses in other countries around the world.

Alpha for Students courses vary in many ways and, even though none looks exactly the same, we want to provide you with a framework around which to work. This manual should help you to understand and put into practice the principles behind the Alpha course while also providing practical guidelines to help maximise the potential of your course no matter how long it has been running.

So, regardless of who you are, we hope that you will read through this manual before you embark upon planning your course and then continue to refer to it as you reach out to students in your area.

Identifying the need

University students are at a unique time of their lives. They face a new environment, new pressures and new challenges that act as a catalyst to their search for answers to the fundamental questions of life. Those who go to university as Christians also face many new challenges and the temptation is often overwhelmingly strong to take advantage of the supposed new freedom that is offered. If they are unsupported the result can be the deterioration of their relationship with God and ultimately a potential loss of faith as the person moves into the working world.

Alpha for Students is targeted specifically at these leaders of tomorrow. It meets the need of both those searching for answers and those who need to strengthen their young faith in Christ. Bringing good news in an accessible and somewhat flexible package, the course allows students a unique chance to hear truth while retaining the freedom to ask questions, explore thoughts and express views that they may be otherwise hesitant to articulate.

Alpha is a tool by which to present the claims of Jesus in a low key but powerful manner to the millions of students who have little or no understanding of the dynamics of the Christian faith.

There are over two million students in the United Kingdom.

Less than 0.5 per cent are estimated to be involved in any Christian expression on campus.

What is Alpha for Students?

Alpha is a 15-session practical introduction to the Christian faith designed primarily for non-churchgoers and new Christians. The syllabus for the course is contained in the book *Questions of Life*. Most courses run in the evening where a light meal is followed by a talk on a subject central to the Christian faith. Students then break into pre-arranged groups (in which they remain for the entire course) to discuss topics raised in an environment where each person should feel free to ask or express whatever they wish. There is also a weekend away in the middle of the course which focuses on the person and work of the Holy Spirit.

It is a low-key, non-threatening course where students from any background or belief system can ask questions about the meaning of life.

Course Content
- *Who Is Jesus?*
- *Why Did Jesus Die?*
- *How Can I Be Sure of My Faith?*
- *Why and How Should I Read the Bible?*
- *Why and How Do I Pray?*
- *How Does God Guide Us?*
- *Who Is the Holy Spirit?**
- *What Does the Holy Spirit Do?**
- *How Can I Be Filled With the Holy Spirit?**
- *How Can I Resist Evil?*
- *Why and How Should We Tell Others?*
- *Does God Heal Today?*
- *What About the Church?*
- *How Can I Make the Most of the Rest of My Life?**

* Material covered during Weekend Away

Plus Introductory Talk
- *Christianity: Boring, Untrue and Irrelevant?*

Why Alpha for Students?

Alpha for Students is just one effective tool for evangelism that is being used to reach out to students around the world. Its main strength lies in its effectiveness in university communities – **the best people to reach students are students.**

Guests are invited along each week by their Christian friends and are introduced into an environment of acceptance, love and respect regardless of their background or spiritual beliefs. During the course they are presented with information about the Christian faith through factual and well-presented talks followed by a place where guests can explore their response in a safe and open forum. Our aim is to bring students into a relationship with God, through Jesus Christ by the power of the Holy Spirit. We hope to make this transition as easy as possible by packaging the gospel in a culturally relevant and accessible way and presenting it to guests as they build relationships in a Christian community – showing them the love that God has for them in words, understanding, experience and reality.

How has Alpha for Students developed?

In 1998 one student decided to try the Alpha course with her friends in her room at university and Alpha for Students was born. There are now over 150[1] Alpha for Students courses running in the UK and it is also running in 25 countries around the world.[2]

---

[1] Courses registered on 1 May 2002

[2] Number of countries known to have student courses as of 1 May 2002

> **Our aim is to introduce Alpha into every university and place of higher education so that every student has the opportunity to attend an Alpha course while they are studying.**

Who is running Alpha for Students?

Students are without doubt the best people to reach their fellow students and invite them on a course. However, Alpha for Students is being effectively run both on and off campus by many different groups of people.

• Student groups

Where the Christian Union, chaplaincy or similar group have decided to run an Alpha for Students course. This can either be on campus, in homes or in a variety of suitable venues outside of the university. It has also proved to be an excellent way of following up a special mission event or week. Various organisations are currently running the course as part of their ongoing yearly programme of evangelism and are feeding new Christians into their existing cell, Bible study or discipleship groups. We have seen groups comprised of undergraduate and postgraduate students and also lecturers running successfully.

• Local churches

A local church may decide to use either an existing Alpha course to reach out to students or set up a new course solely for those studying in their area. These courses are most often run off campus while scheduled to fit into an academic term. They are advertised on campus and have small groups designated for students led by students.

Some churches have also provided a venue or speakers for a course while encouraging students to invite their friends along and to lead the small groups. Local church support has proved invaluable when planning the weekends away and providing continuity for the follow-up of new Christians – students value the support and the partnership is vital.

• Students in their homes

Two or three students may decide to run the course in their rooms to reach out to their immediate group of friends. It is the most natural thing to invite your friends round for a meal, to watch a video and to discuss it over coffee.

Chapter 1

Deciding whether you can do it

Is this ever going to happen?

Who will be on your team?

Before you start to plan your new Alpha for Students course it is a really good idea to think about who will run it with you. Are you alone in your excitement to reach out to the students in your area or are you potentially surrounded by a wonderful team?

What is your situation?
If you are a student...

- Are you a part of a wider Christian group?
- What Christian friends do you have at your university or in your church?
- What Christian groups/organisations are active on your campus?
- Do you have a chaplain at your university?
- Is there support available within any of your local churches?

Try to approach as many of the above as possible and to share with them your vision and ideas for Alpha for Students at your university. If you belong to a group this would be a good time to talk to your committee or leadership team and ask them to put the weight of the whole group behind the course.

You can ask them to consider supporting you in the following ways:

Invitation – asking them to publicise the course and encourage their friends to come along.

Time – having people committed to the course every week.

Prayer – praying for the course each week.

Finances – they may be able to give you some money to help cover expenses.

Talks – if you plan to use live speakers they might have suitable and experienced people.
The more support you can get – the better!

If you are a local church...

- Do you have any students in your church?
- Do you have people of student age in your church?
- What support do you have from the wider congregation of the church?

To reach students you need students involved in leading your course. It is a great idea to recruit help from regular members of the congregation but is absolutely essential that students lead the small groups for students. This is because students will discuss issues at a different pace and in a different way to other adults. It is a good idea to make the group as natural for them as possible. If the leaders are recent students or of student age then this is also preferable to having older individuals leading their discussions.

You will also need students to support and publicise your Alpha for Students course from within the university. Key students within the church may be able to contact Christians from the university (see list above for '*If you are a student*') to ask for support.

If you are a student worker or chaplain...

As with the two categories above, consider who will work with you, ask for help and support from all of the groups mentioned and make sure that you have students on your team.

Your target audience: How will you get students on your course?

Consider the potential size of your course. Who are you running your course for? Are you trying to reach your corridor, your hall of residence, your whole university? How will you get word out about the course?

It is true that the more publicity you have the better *(see Chapter 4)*. However, the key to getting people on the course is always **personal invitation**. The questions you need to ask yourself at this point are 'Who is likely to come?' and 'How will I ask them?' One factor that will always directly affect the size of your course is the number of people you have on your team. In our experience most courses attract guests at a maximum ratio of three guests per one team member, although it is sometimes lower than this. It is ideal if you and your team know many non-Christians. If you feel that you are limited in this area it would be advisable to think through ways that you can personally invite guests and how you can get other supporting groups to ask their friends and colleagues along.

Resources: What will you need?

Alpha for Students courses can be run at very little cost *(see Appendix B)*. However, it is still good to consider where any funding required will come from. Influencing factors to be considered are as follows:

- Is it likely that you will have to pay for room hire?
- Will you charge for any meal/food served and will you need to subsidise it?
- Can you borrow any materials (eg videos) or will you have to purchase everything yourself?
- How much are you willing to pay for a weekend

away? Will you need to subsidise guests?
- Will you require an 'appetiser' event to kick off your course? This may require funds.

How can I finance my course?

Alpha for Students is an evangelistic course that will reach out to students with the gospel. It is the type of event that some churches or individuals (both student and non-student) might be keen to support financially. The key to this usually is simply asking and letting people know that you have a need. This gives people the opportunity to pray about whether they feel it right to give you some money. Some students involved in your course may like the chance to contribute to the expenses and it is a good idea to give them the chance to do so.

See Chapter 17 for more help in this area.

Students running an Alpha for Students course in the UK receive a 67 per cent discount on all Alpha resources.

Practical issues of Alpha for Students

Here are some other practical questions to ask yourself as you decide whether to run an Alpha for Students course:

1. Venue
Where will you hold the course each week?
Ideally the best venue would be one that fulfilled the

following criteria – the more you can satisfy, the better the venue:

- With catering facilities (to cater for a meal and/or warm drinks etc.)

- Near to your target area of students (where they will be at the time the course is running).

- Comfortable room (or with potential to make it comfortable and relaxing).

- Good amenities, eg well lit and warm etc.

- Accessible and easy to find (not hidden).

- Reasonably well known location.

- Low cost or no cost!

- Available to be used each week at the same time (without having to move rooms).

- No restrictive rules, eg 'No food or drink' or 'No music'.

- Quiet and uninterrupted location, eg that room isn't needed for access to other rooms.

- Privacy – some guests may not want to be on display as they join your course.

- With good facilities as needed, such as OHP, screen, PA, music system, TV and video.

2. Food
Do you want to provide a meal each week?

It can appear easier to miss out the recommended meal from your Alpha for Students course. However, we strongly recommend that you try to include this positive ingredient of the course in any way possible. If you come across stumbling blocks to challenge you, these ideas may help you to think through your options.

- **Full meal**

Alpha for Students does not demand an elaborate feast – a simple main course followed by fruit or something similar is perfectly adequate for your guests. If your course is small you may decide to take it in turns to cook. Or for a larger course you could have a team of volunteers to look after the catering as a group or take it in turns each week. It is also worth asking local churches to help you prepare and transport your meal if you are struggling to find competent and willing chefs! There is an *Alpha Cookbook* available *(see Appendix B)* to suggest menu ideas that are cheap and easy when catering for large or small numbers. Paper plates and plastic cutlery can be used to save labour and reduce mess. If cost is an issue – it is absolutely fine to ask guests for a recommended donation to cover the cost.

- **Snack**

If you are planning a course at lunch times, perhaps sandwiches or lighter snacks may be more suitable. This will reduce the preparation time and take slightly less time out of your session while still allowing the vital interaction and relationship building that take place while eating.

- **Dessert**

Do your target guests live in catered accommodation or do you feel that that the timing of your course would suggest that most people would have already eaten? Is it impossible to get around the obstacles of having a full meal for whatever reason? You may like to consider having a dessert as the 'food' component of Alpha for Students.

Without having a full meal it is still possible for you to offer a dessert of some kind together with coffee or hot chocolate. You can use your imagination in this area and come up with an attractive alternative that would still allow your guests, group leaders and helpers to mingle and get to know each other.

- **Coffee and cake**

If all else fails try a cup of coffee and a slice of cake or biscuits. If you make this an important feature in your course each session, it could still be a very useful time. It is always preferable to have a main meal as part of your course but if this is not possible having coffee and cake is still worth the effort.

Venue and food – a combined solution

An alternative solution for both of these areas would be to consider holding your course in a different type of venue.

Restaurant

Ask local cheap restaurants if they might consider letting you use a back room (check that you have control as to who uses it when you are there). They cater while you eat and continue your course effortlessly.

Pub or coffee shop

Either of these may have a room you could use but do check that you won't be interrupted unnecessarily. They may have a kitchen or be able to cater to your needs alongside their usual activities. This has proven to be a great venue for several courses in the UK. These are natural habitats for students where they feel very at home.

3. Timing

There are three questions to be asked here.

What time of day?
What day of the week?
Which weeks of the year?

Time

Your options are basically as follows:

Morning – for breakfast

Lunch – for snack time

Evening (or early evening) – for a meal or other refreshments (This option has proved to be the most popular)

Choose whichever works best for both team and guests.

Day

Pick a day that:

a)   Is convenient to you and your team throughout the whole course.

b)   Avoids potential clashes with big and regular student events each week.

c)   Avoids other church or campus group meeting nights (unless agreed that you will replace regular meetings with Alpha).

Weeks

To cater for students it is essential that you run the course within term time.

The first thing to do is to plan in advance and find out when your university terms start and finish – use these as guidelines when you plan your dates.

Short terms

There are many options for fitting your course into your term.

See Appendix C for suggested programmes for 8, 9 or 10 week terms.

Can you run Alpha over two terms with a break in the middle?

From experience we would always advise you to fit your course into one term. This may involve extra planning near the end of a previous term to start immediately in the new term but it is very worthwhile.

If it is impossible to use the suggested timings for your course then splitting it over two terms may be the only option. In such circumstances it is always preferable to plan your weekend during the first term. The aim would be to build strong friendships before you disappear for the holidays to ensure as much as possible that people will return to finish the course after the break.

Mini Alpha courses

If you find yourself with an exceptionally short period of time and still want to run Alpha for Students, please contact the Alpha for Students Office for specific advice. The course is essentially 10 weeks in length and any major changes in its structure may dramatically affect its effectiveness. In this instance – please seek our advice.

Now you should be in a position to decide whether Alpha for Students is possible within your hall, university, group, Christian Union, chaplaincy, church or home.

We hope that you feel encouraged to get started – so let's get the show on the road.

Chapter 2

Getting the ball rolling

How to administrate your Alpha for Students course

Before you begin the exciting business of getting your course organised and immersed in administration, remind yourself about your overall aims in running an Alpha for Students course.

You will be facilitating a course intended to bring students into a relationship with Christ. Put yourself in the shoes of each guest to ensure that you look after them thoroughly and remove every possible obstacle to the gospel.

- From the moment they walk through the door into your course everything around them (including Christians and the environment) will represent Christ to them. We need to make sure that we represent him well in everything we do, say and organise. We want each guest to feel welcome, comfortable and well cared for while they are with us, to show that the course is a good use of their time and that we are happy for them to be with us.

- Many of your guests will arrive with a stereotypical view of Christianity and everything connected with it. For example, they may have been exposed to religion in many contexts. Most of these environments undoubtedly will have been unnatural and unpleasant habitats for them. We want to break any such misconceptions about the Christian community and demonstrate to them that they can feel relaxed and at home with us. We want them to concentrate, reflect, and be open and willing to enter into discussion about their spirituality and beliefs.

Bearing this in mind – we can continue to get things moving.

Appoint an administrator

Quite surprisingly, this isn't as scary as it sounds. Every course requires a multi-talented individual who is able to throw themselves into getting the course established and then keeping it going.

You are looking for someone with the following resources, skills and attitudes:

- **Enthusiasm**
  Someone who wants to do the job

- **Time**
  It won't be all consuming but they will need to be able to fit it in to their schedule

- **Energy**
  To keep going when challenges arise

- **Sense of humour**
  The ability to laugh and enjoy the ride

- **Interpersonal skills**
  Must enjoy people – from registering them on the first night to pastoral chats

- **Ability to delegate**
  To be able to ask others to do something and then trust that they will without worrying

- **Ability to work well on all levels**
  Behind the scenes and front of house

- **Highly organised**
  Very important – To have many balls in the air at one time and not to drop them! Ability to run one course, plan the next and be preparing for the one after

After reading this list you will know whether or not this is you. If it isn't then you will need to appoint someone else to work with you as you lead the course. If it is you, congratulations! You have earned yourself a job and it will be a lot of fun.

Register your course

This is VERY important and very easy to do:

1. **Post** – complete an Alpha for Students Registration Form and return it to the Alpha for Students Office (see Appendix A)

2. **Online** – visit **alphacourse.org**

3. **Telephone** – call the Alpha for Students Office (see Appendix A)

You will then receive the following benefits:

- For students running courses in the UK – a **67 per cent discount** on all Alpha resources ordered through STL (UK distributors of Alpha resources).

- Your course will be listed in the Alpha Course Directory. This can be accessed online at alphacourse.org or listings can be seen in Alpha News.

This enables students looking for a course at or near their university to see which courses are available and to make contact with you.

- **The Alpha for Students Office** will be able to support, guide and pray for your course. We always love to hear how your courses are going and to help you in any way we can (see Appendix A).

Set your dates

We recommend that you consider your course schedule in terms of the academic year as a whole.

Alpha works at its best when part of a rolling programme of evangelism. This means as one course is ending the next course has been planned and the momentum is constantly maintained. You will have to discover the best way of doing this at your institution having taken your term or semester dates into consideration.

An ideal rolling programme might look something like one of the following options:

- A two semester academic year – two courses
- A three term academic year – two or three courses

See 'Timing' section of Chapter 1 to help you plan specific course timings.

As you set your dates it is useful to consider who will make up your team. While helping on an Alpha course is great fun, it also demands commitment and energy from those involved. Ideally you would be looking to recruit new team members from the Christian graduates of your courses.

The best people to become helpers on a new course are those who have recently started their relationship with Christ and have been filled with the Holy Spirit.

They are enthusiastic and excited about God and will bring both their freshness and their friends to your next course. The great thing about this is that you are constantly preventing burnout in your team because you have an increasingly broad pool of people from which to recruit after each course. This is not to say that long time Christians cannot repeatedly be a part of your course. The opposite is true in fact – as your course grows you will need lots of help. However, the best way to run a successful course is to ensure that you have a trained and willing team and not an exhausted and overworked group. It is also a good idea to train another administrator and leader to take over the course when you need a break yourself.

Team (leaders and helpers)

The most important thing to consider is:

Who do you want on your team?

When setting up a course, it is usual for several people to volunteer themselves into key roles. Before you know it, you have a full team but have had virtually no real choice in selecting your team.

We recommend that on every course, the leaders pick the people they want to INVITE to become leaders and helpers. This is how they come to that decision:

The test

Think of a friend who you have been praying for over a very long period of time and then imagine that they want to come on your Alpha course. Would you be happy to leave them in the hands of your chosen leader?

If the answer is no, then we would suggest that this is perhaps the wrong person to be leading or helping on your course. This is a great rule of thumb by which to make your choice.

Who will fit this high standard?

The type of person you are looking for should possess as many of the following skills as possible:

Outgoing	Caring
Patient	Sense of humour
Confident	Capable of relaxed conversation
Sensitive	
Relates well to everyone	Ability to lead
Committed	Enthusiastic
Good fun	

The list could be endless. Basically you are searching for almost perfect people!

The leaders and helpers you choose need not have been Christians for a very long time – if they are enthusiastic and fit the other criteria then they will go on a very sharp learning curve but will undoubtedly do a great job. They do not need to be great theologians or have vast spiritual maturity to help or lead in a small group. If a person has been a Christian for just a few months they will make a great helper and will be able to bring their honesty and openness to benefit the group enormously.

One more thing worth emphasising to your potential team is the commitment required throughout Alpha. You should encourage your team to block every Alpha session out in their diaries. Your small groups will depend upon your team being there each week, during the weekend away and also at all the training sessions. Your team should be asked to commit to the whole course.

See Chapter 1 for ideas on where to find people to help you.

Core Team

Even though you may invite people to join your team, you will undoubtedly still have volunteers who are keen to help out with the course in any way they can. This is just what you need to make your course run even better – volunteers to make up your 'Core Team'.

For those who aren't as confident or ready to be either a leader or a helper in a group, there is a still a great deal to be done. Your Core Team is an essential part of your course. They will take care of things that make each Alpha session happen:

• Setting up your venue
• Preparing and serving food
• Clearing up after the meal
• Serving tea and coffee etc
• Clearing up at the end of the session

Your Core Team will be the first people into your venue each week and the last people to leave. They allow you to concentrate on the guests each week and free you to ensure that everything goes smoothly.

For small courses you will need one or two members in your Core Team. As your course increases in size you will need more people to help. It is advisable to ask one person to head the team and to ensure that every area of duty is looked after.

There should be time each week for your Core Team to meet together and pray – perhaps during the talk or video. One idea is to invite them along on the weekend or day away as guests. They will really enjoy joining in with the fun and also to have the opportunity to be ministered to and to pray for each other.

Regardless of the size of your course, your Core Team is precious to you. Take care of them and treat them well. We all have valuable gifts and skills to bring to an Alpha team and, no matter the role, every person is an integral part of the course and team.

Choose your venue

At this point you should confirm your venue.

If you are booking rooms on campus you will need to be aware of the regulations and timings for your booking requests to be submitted. Some Students' Unions and universities will not confirm bookings until the beginning of a new term and semester. This could affect your advertising, as you will be unable to detail where the course will be held. If this happens, it may be a good idea to prepare well in advance. You could produce a first batch of invitations stating that the venue is to be confirmed and provide a contact address for potential guests to find out at a later date. As soon as the booking is confirmed, you should print a second batch of advertising with posters and fliers displayed clearly and prominently to ensure that those who are interested know where to go.

See Chapter 1 for help in finding a good venue

Invite your guests

The most effective way of attracting guests to your course is through personal invitation. The course invitation is a useful tool for this.

You can either use one of the standard Alpha for Students invitations and personalise them with your course details or you can create your own. Whichever route you choose, it is advisable to have large numbers of invitations available for all your team and friends to distribute freely. Get them produced well in advance, especially if you are holding a celebration event at the end of your course, because they are a very effective tool to advertise and promote the dates of the next course.

We will look at more methods of advertising in Chapter 4 'Getting People There'.

Small groups

This is where the real work of Alpha goes on.

Training

Ensure that every leader and helper on your course has completed all the training material. If any members of your team are unable to go through the Alpha training then it may be worth finding alternative people to take over their roles for that course. The model Alpha small group is unlike most Christian enquiry courses, which makes it imperative that every person on the team has the same vision for the type of group they want and has learned the skills to make that happen. Regardless of how many times your leaders and helpers have been involved in Alpha

or any other course, we would advise that the whole team completes the training each time.

As the course administrator, organise a time when your team might do the training together. It is also an opportunity to get everyone together before the course begins to build team spirit and pray for your course and each other.

See Chapter 5 for more information about training your leaders and helpers.

Setting up for groups

Your venue should be set up with approximately 12 chairs in a circle for each of your small groups. They will remain in this set up for the whole evening unless you have insufficient space for the discussions to take place in which case you may need an overflow room also set up for some groups. The most important thing to remember is that your groups should stick together throughout the evening.

Putting the groups together

This is usually a last minute task. Ideally your guests would pre-register for the course but generally students will just turn up on the night and you will have to allocate them groups when they walk through the door.

- **The small group model**
You are aiming to have groups that contain the following:

    1–2 leaders
    1–2 helpers
    8–12 guests

The maximum number of people for your groups should be no more than 12–15 (undoubtedly some guests will drop out or miss weeks).

Your group leaders and helpers should always be students or of student age.

- **Group hopping**

Occasionally a situation may arise when guests may want to switch groups mid-course. This will work early in the course (up to Week 4) although it is good to discourage unless there is a very good reason. If someone wants to move groups more than once, try chatting to them and persuade them to stay where they are. Group hopping can be disruptive to the relationships already being formed in the new group and often hurtful to those in the old. It is quite unusual for there to be a genuine reason for guests to move and is often only due to seeing or hearing other groups that can appear to be having more fun.

- **Preparation**

You will need to estimate how many groups you will need before the course begins. However, as your guests arrive, you need to fill one group at a time and then move on to the next group when that one is full.

Prepare for this by arranging to have someone register each person immediately upon arrival. Have a sheet of paper for each group. When your guest arrives ask them their name and how they heard about the course. Then allocate them to a group and write their name on the appropriate piece of paper. This way you will have a list of the members of each group and also know when you have filled its group. Ask guests for a contact e-mail address or phone number. This is not

for you to use to chase them up each week but is just for emergency situations when you might need to advise them of a change of room or something similar. Explain this to the guest to put their mind at rest and if they are unhappy to give you any details do not pressurise them in any way.

Appoint a treasurer

It is always important to keep a clear financial account of course expenditure, especially if you receive any support from outside groups, churches or people. If you are running a small course you may be able to look after the finances yourself but if your course is slightly larger it may be advisable to ask someone else on your team to be your treasurer.

Planning the weekend or day away

The earlier you set your dates for the weekend or day the better.

The best time to arrange it is between Weeks 5 and 7. It is preferable to have the talk 'How Can I Resist Evil?' in the session immediately after you return. You may need to change your talk order slightly to achieve this.

Telling your guests

In Week 3 you will need to advertise the weekend. The course leader should inform all the team and encourage the individual group leaders to promote it to their guests. A good way of doing this is for the leader to chat with the most enthusiastic guest in their small group to cheer them along into coming on the weekend. At the beginning of the discussion group, the leader can mention the weekend and refer to the enthusiastic person saying '… you are going to come aren't you?' Hopefully this will encourage other members of the group to come as they are inevitably more likely to attend with people they know.

It is also helpful if the leader writes a cheque to pay for the weekend in front of the group, as this will reassure others into doing the same. If anyone is having any difficulties in making the weekend or day try to gently persuade them to get round their obstacles and pray that they would be able to make it.

See Chapter 8 for more detailed help.

Appetiser events

The appetiser event is the best way to get your course started if you have either never run Alpha for Students before or if you have had a break since your last course.

To get everything started

Try to be creative with the appetiser event and have a lot of fun. Plan everything well in advance, ensure that the event is promoted as early as possible and encouraging all the students you know to invite their friends. Have a large number of invitations available to be distributed widely for the event.

An Alpha appetiser would usually comprise either a meal or some entertainment with a break for one or two testimonies from people who have come to faith on Alpha. This would be followed by a short evangelistic talk, such as 'Christianity: Boring, Untrue and Irrelevant?'. At the end of the talk there is an open invitation to the next Alpha for Students course. Each guest should be given an invitation leaflet and *Why Jesus?* booklets (or *Why Christmas?*) should also be available.

Your event will vary in size or content according to how many people you have helping on your course. Try to have an appetiser that bears some relation to the size and atmosphere of the course that will follow it. Eg if you are planning a small course in your hall of residence room you would not want to organise an event for 400 in the main bar of the Students' Union.

See Chapter 6 for more information about how to set up an appetiser or celebration event.

Questionnaires

Everyone has groaned at one time or another when presented with a questionnaire regardless of where it has come from. However, as the Alpha course has been repeatedly run and developed over the years, the questionnaire has proved to be one of the most helpful tools in moving the course forward. From it you will learn how people felt about the different aspects of your course: the things they enjoyed the most and the parts they found the most difficult. You will also have the privilege of hearing stories and testimonies of how the course has helped your guests move on in their spiritual journeys.

Distribute the questionnaires on the last session of your course and ask guests to complete them at the beginning of their small group time. Collect them there and then, read them well and prayerfully consider how you might want to make some alterations to make your next course the best ever.

See Appendix G for a sample questionnaire.

Thanks

As discussed earlier, Alpha always works best when run by a team of people. Whether your team is small or large it is essential to appreciate your fellow workers. Remember to thank regularly everyone involved. Prayer times are a great time to keep showing encouragement and appreciation and don't forget also to thank your Core Team who will be working continuously behind the scenes.

A celebration event at the end of the course or a reunion evening after the course can also be a good way of publicly saying thank you to those who have worked with you.

Chapter 3
And so the course starts
The first night

Prayer and administration meeting

While your Core Team set up your venue each week, gather all your leaders and helpers together. For the first two weeks you may need slightly more time to cover everything. Start by meeting one hour before the guests arrive, then reduce it to 45 minutes and then to 30 minutes once the course is in full swing.

Issues to cover

You may want to start with worship and prayer to get everyone focused.

Prayer

- for guests to come along and be open to what they hear

- for the speaker (if you have live talks)

- for the leaders and helpers

- for the Core Team

- for the logistics and technical arrangements

- for God to bless the course

Plus any other issues or challenges that your course may be facing.

Your course leader should chat briefly through the issues that might be raised in the talk and briefly discuss any questions that are likely to arise.

Administration

On about Week 3, the leader will start to advertise the weekend or day away after they have welcomed the guests and told a joke. In the team meeting you should discuss how this will be handled in the small group and how places can be reserved and money paid (*see Chapter 8 for more help*).

You may also use this time to keep your team up to date with plans for any celebration events, subsequent courses and when the third training session will be held.

Feedback

Have a short feedback time about highlights or matters for prayer that arose the previous week. This should be encouraging and helpful as the team pulls together to support each other throughout the course.

It is most important that your meeting finishes in time for the leaders and helpers to be ready and seated in their small groups waiting for their guests to arrive.

Welcome team

For your first two weeks you will need a few more volunteers than usual to form your welcome team.

You will need to decide how large your team should be; however, it is always preferable to have more people than needed rather than too few. Your welcome team members should be positioned to welcome guests and make them feel totally welcome and at ease from the moment they walk through the door. They will be the first point of contact for most of your guests and therefore need to be smiling and inviting to everyone.

After your guests have registered you will also need a couple of people from your welcome team to take them to their groups and introduce them to the group leaders. The aim here is to ensure that no guest is left feeling self-conscious or alone at any point. All conversations should be kept light and non-spiritual. Show interest in your guests and at all times be available for their needs.

Name labels

For the first few weeks have simple labels with your guests' first names written clearly in black marker pen.

This may seem a little false but is well worth doing because it will help you get to know your guests by name and also make it easier for them to remember yours. Try not to rely on the name labels too much since you should stop using them after Week 3.

Alpha manuals

Provide manuals to give to each guest on their first visit. The manual is theirs to keep and make notes in.

Some of your guests may leave the manuals at the end of the night. Leave some of the spares in every small group after the first week.

Bibles

If you are able, provide each group with enough Bibles for guests to refer to during the talks. If everyone uses the group Bibles your guests will not feel any different and this will help avoid any Christian/non-Christian divide.

The meal

Your food should be available at the start of the evening when the guests arrive. Encourage your leaders and helpers to assist their group by taking them to get their meal and to make sure they have everything they need.

Cost

It is okay to ask for a suggested donation for food on your course. Place a bowl where guests collect their food with a sign detailing how much you would recommend they contribute. If you are going to charge for food it is advisable to detail this on your course invitations and advertising. Keep it simple and relatively inexpensive.

See Chapter 1 for more information on how to use food on your course.

Introduction, worship and talk/video

After the meal is over and the Core Team has cleared away it is time to start the talk.

Introduction

The course leader should welcome everyone to the course and tell a joke to put the guests at ease.

See Appendix J for some joke ideas.

Worship

It is completely up to you whether to include worship on your course although we do recommend it if at all possible.

For courses with less than 12 people it is more likely that you will choose not to since singing is not a normal activity for most students. When making your decision consider how your guests will feel. The fewer the people the harder it is to sing in a group. In larger groups the worship is slightly more anonymous and will therefore be a little easier for guests.

It is worth noting that having worship throughout your course can be both the worst thing and the best thing for many guests who come on Alpha. The first few weeks are usually a little embarrassing but when you get to your weekend or day away you will reap the benefits of having your guests already used to worship. If you have not used worship, your guests might feel slightly uncomfortable.

If you have decided to use worship on your course now is the time for your worship leader to start the singing. Stick closely to the Alpha recipe for worship because it can be a particularly tricky part of the evening for your guests and it is important to make it as accessible for them as possible.

See Appendix F and Chapter 10 for help with your worship planning.

Talk/video
Immediately after worship launch straight into the video or talk. It is important that you do not present this section with a lengthy introduction, nor should you add to the content by doing a short talk after the video or speaker.

Coffee, biscuits and small group discussions
Immediately after the video or speaker has finished, group leaders and helpers should serve coffee or other drinks and biscuits to their group. This will again put

the group at ease and help them move into the small group discussion.

The group should always end on time according to the programme.

Bookshop
Although it is not essential, we would recommend that you have some books available for your guests and team to purchase.

These are perhaps the most important books to have:

BOOKS	BOOKLETS
Questions of Life	*What About Other Religions?*
Searching Issues	*Why Jesus?*
30 Days	*Why Does God Allow Suffering?*

The Alpha manual suggests some reading after each session for those who are interested in finding out more about that topic. For most student courses it is impossible to have all these books available each week without spending a large amount of money. However, if any of your guests are interested in reading further, it is worthwhile helping them because most will not be aware of Christian bookshops or where they might purchase what they require.

Chapter 4

Getting people there
Publicity strategies – ideas

Over the years it has become clear that the majority of people who attend an Alpha course are there because they have received a **personal invitation**.

On the first night of Alpha we recommend that each leader go around their small group to ask how each guest has come to be on the course. Invariably, the most common answer is that they are there because a friend, colleague, relative or acquaintance has invited them along. The same is proving to be true with Alpha for Students.

The people who are the most effective at getting their friends and college course mates along are those who have just done Alpha for Students and become Christians as a result. They are natural walking advertisements! Encourage and support them as they tell their friends what has happened.

Take advantage of the brand

This is not to say that advertising other than the personal invitation is not important – in fact the opposite is true. As the number of Alpha courses has increased, particularly in the UK, we have witnessed a huge rise in awareness of Alpha. This is the cumulative effect of word of mouth and annual advertising campaigns that have appeared on billboards, the backs of buses, countless church notice boards and various newspaper, radio and television interviews and reports that have been published or broadcast.

When planning your course it is a good idea to take advantage of other Alpha publicity. The main national advertising campaign takes place to support the annual Alpha Initiative. Contact the Alpha for Students Office to find out when the initiative will take place and schedule the promotion of your course to fit with the wider advertising that will be happening.

Every poster you put up, advert you place, every event you run or invitation you distribute is supporting and reinforcing PERSONAL INVITATIONS that will be made for students to attend your course.

Alpha for Students resources

There are several ways in which we can help you in your advertising programme.

Alpha for Students Course Directory

As soon as you know you will be running a course you should register yourself with the Alpha for Students Office. This will place your course on a listing both in *Alpha News* and on the website course directory. If any students from your area are searching for a course they are sure to looking for one of these two places where they will find your contact details and be able to come along.

See Appendix H for a course Registration Form. For alternative ways to register see Chapter 2 'Register your course'.

Invitations and posters

There are Alpha for Students invitations and posters for you to purchase on which you can print your own course details or, alternatively, you can create your own designs as long as you use the Alpha logo somewhere on all promotional material. You can obtain the logo from alphacourse.org.

Drinks mats

These are a fantastic resource that you can print or stamp your course details on. Use them as give-aways for your fresher stall or as invitations. Students will often hang on to a mat to keep on their desk. You could also to distribute them around your campus cafés, bars and common areas.

For UK courses, Alpha resources can be ordered from STL (UK distributors). If you are outside the UK, please contact the Alpha for Students Office for advice on how to order.

See Appendix B for more details about ordering Alpha for Students resources.

Take advantage of your own resources

Each campus, church and every person involved with your team will present you with some skill or opportunity to utilise in your advertising campaign. Take a good look at what and who is around you and make sure that you take advantage of every chance to inform people about what you are planning. Following are a few ideas as you consider what resources may be at your fingertips.

Local or university radio and news publications

Investigate both of these options. Tell them about what you are doing with special reference to any unusual public events that you are planning.

- People love to hear or read about the lives of others. You may find that real life stories are a powerful way of communicating what it is all about.

- If you are running a large musical event you may want to invite the stations to broadcast it!

- Some Students' Unions print diary sheets in their campus magazines detailing all the events of the coming week.

One thing to be aware of is that you will rarely have control over the slant that journalists may report from and you should be careful wherever possible not to be misquoted or misrepresented especially when in print.

Inform other churches and societies

Always remember to excite and envision students from local churches, the Christian Union and other societies to ask their non-Christian friends along too.

You could also contact other non-Christian societies to let them know that they will be welcome to come along too. You may need to do this sensitively, but you could invite other religious groups along. This works especially well if you or someone on your team is a good friend with a member of another group or society – you could send them an e-mail and ask them to forward it to their friends.

Campus advertising opportunities

Be creative as you consider your campus. Can you post invitations into departmental pigeonholes? Do you have access to put drink mats in any of your campus venues? Can you project an advertisement on the side of a central building?

Create your own website

Believe it or not, creating a website can take as little as five minutes and cost you absolutely nothing. There are loads of 'free' sites on the web that are available to make a simple but funky site.

Having a course website can be an excellent and cheap way of informing potential guests about your course. If you are part of a registered society, it is usually quite easy to get linked in from your university or college website. If you have a little more time to spend on designing your site, it has the potential to be an effective way of attracting students to your course.

Events

• Freshers' Week

This is possibly the biggest opportunity in the academic year to invite almost every first year student to your Alpha for Students course. Apply early to the Students' Union to get a stall (you may need to be a registered society but it is always worth enquiring as early as possible). Then be creative! Make sure it is eye-catching and will make an impact on those passing by. Have plenty of invitations ready and a team of willing, confident, enthusiastic students to chat to people as they go past. Free gift bags are always an attraction. You could include Alpha invitations together with pens, drink mats, sweets or whatever else you can come up with and it is always good to have some *Why Jesus?* booklets available.

• Appetiser events

You could organise an event to launch your course and publicise it well. Consider the time of year, the location, what else is going on and what would really appeal to the students you are hoping to attract.

Following are suggestions of appetiser events that have worked well for Alpha for Students courses.

Carol services – Christmas is a perfect opportunity to attract students seeking a little tradition. Use is as an appetiser for your course. Check to see if you can work with your campus chapel or a local church to run a special student service. Testimonies work really well in this environment, especially if you can get one or two that have become Christians on Alpha (*see Chapter 6 for more help on how to use testimonies*). Also you could invite a speaker to deliver the *Why Christmas?* talk (a seasonal version of 'Christianity: Boring, Untrue and Irrelevant?' evangelistic talk). Always have a good supply of the *Why Christmas?* or *Why Jesus?* booklets and Alpha invitations for everyone.

Event in the Students' Union – Try planning a Jazz evening, club night, 70s disco, BBQ, band night or whatever else you think would appeal. Again you can use testimonies and the short evangelistic talk 'Christianity: Boring, Untrue and Irrelevant?', with an open invitation to your new course (have postcard invitations freely available).

Meal in your home/halls of residence/church – This is much more informal but equally effective if you are planning a smaller course. Invite many friends around for a special meal. Take some time to make the evening a little different and memorable for your guests, eg you could hold a theme dinner or a murder mystery evening. You might consider a talk a little too much for such an evening; a testimony from one of the guests about their experience on Alpha may be perfect for that environment. Ensure that everyone knows they are invited to come on the course and have invitations for them to take away with all the details.

Mission events – Your Christian Union, church or other mission event would be fantastic to launch your course and encourage people along. If your CU or any other groups on campus are planning to run outreach events or socials, ask them to use the event to advertise your new Alpha for Students course, even if the event is not specifically a designated Alpha Appetiser.

See Chapter 13 for help on using Alpha with mission events.

Pre-Alpha guest service – You could work with your local church or campus chapel to hold a special guest service the Sunday before your Alpha for Students course begins. A suitable programme for the guest service should include two or three testimonies from students who have recently become Christians on Alpha and a low-key evangelistic talk. Encourage people to invite their friends to the service as a taster to the upcoming course. This type of event works well alongside another more 'fun' appetiser.

See Chapter 6 on how to use testimonies effectively.

These are just some ideas to get you started. You will probably think of some other amazing and original ideas to get the word out that your course is starting soon.

Chapter 5

Getting your team ready

Training essentials

At this point in your preparation it is good to remind both yourself and your team why you are running the course and, more importantly, to equip all of you to run the course. This is where the training fits in.

If you remember only one thing from this entire manual, let it be this:

Always cover all the training

Training is vital for every single person of your team to communicate the aims of Alpha and the method to achieve it. Just as we want to break our guests' stereotypical image of Christianity we also want to break our own traditional behaviour when faced with a Bible study, Christian enquiry group or worldviews debate.

The training will give your team the heart and desire to love guests that come on the course and also provide them with practical ways to do this.

The place where it all happens

Leading a small group on Alpha, whatever your role, is very different from leading any other type of Christian small group. This is the place where a real difference is made and it is essential that people clearly understand their role.

The model Alpha small group

The model Alpha small group is not a 'speaker–audience' situation and neither is it a 'teacher–pupil' scenario. The atmosphere to promote is that of 'host–guest'. Quite simply, each leader should act as if their guests are present in their own home (in fact they may well be). Every person should be treated with dignity, respect and honour in a group that is low-key, unpressurised and non-confrontational. It is a safe place for guests to discuss their beliefs, thoughts or questions without being judged, laughed at or criticised.

The skills needed to nurture this environment are demonstrated during the training. Your team will receive direct guidelines as to their role:

- **Leaders lead** – deflecting questions and promoting pleasant discussion.

- **Helpers help** – saying nothing during discussion time and playing host at all other times.

Your team will be encouraged about when and how to model Bible study and prayer. They will understand that it is vital to move at the pace of the slowest person in their group and to release them into a relationship of reading the Bible and praying for themselves.

The result will be a team of encouragers and listeners who will set about building lasting friendships with potentially new members of the body of Christ. The refreshing thing about the training is that it will give your team confidence to let God do the work throughout the course as they simply show his love to those who attend. This way, the Christians will enjoy the course feeling more equipped and prepared; envisioned and excited; challenged and committed. It is an exciting process to watch.

Practical training

Session One – Leading Small Groups

Session Two – Pastoral Care

Session Three – Ministry

You will need to plan either two or three sessions for your training. Training is available on video or audio and it is recommended that the whole team go through it together. This will build relationships within the team before the course starts and allow time for discussion, planning and prayer.

The first two training sessions can be done separately or together in one evening. Why not make your training sessions into a social evening? Have a meal together followed by the first training session, break for coffee and dessert and then watch the second video. You can end the evening by praying for your course and each other (the third session need not be watched until the week before your Weekend Away). A suggested timetable for your first training evening might be as follows:

6.30pm	Meal
7.15pm	Worship
7.30pm	Training session 1 – 'Leading Small Groups'
8.15pm	Coffee break
8.30pm	Training session 2 – 'Pastoral Care'
9.15pm	Prayer and worship
10.00pm	End

Since this would be a long evening, you could do the training on two separate occasions, although it would still be good to pray together on either one or both occasions.

The third session is ideally watched during the week before your weekend or day away. Again, follow it with prayer, especially for one another to model the prayer ministry that will occur on the weekend itself.

Time permitting, another useful training point would be to suggest your team try to read *Searching Issues* and *Telling Others* (both by Nicky Gumbel) to prepare them even more for some of the topics that may arise throughout the course.

Even if you have done the training repeatedly, it is still important to refresh your memory by re-training with the rest of your team each time the course commences.

Manuals

Each member of your team will need a copy of the *Alpha Team Training Manual*. This will help them to follow the training sessions and to make their own notes. The manual also contains ideas to refer to throughout the course to aid discussion and possible Bible studies.

Why not make your training sessions into a social evening? Watch the first session on video followed by a meal together. Afterwards, watch the second video and then pray for your course and each other (the third session need not be watched until the week before your Weekend Away).

Live speakers

Even more preferable to the videos would be a live speaker to do your training. This can then be condensed slightly and made directly applicable to

your student environment. Anyone delivering the
training talks should follow the points in the training
material exactly and would need to be very familiar
with Alpha, having been involved in the course on
many occasions.

*If you require help with finding someone to lead your
training, please contact your Alpha Advisor or the Alpha
for Students Office for ideas (see Appendix A).*

Chapter 6

And so it begins

Planning an appetiser event

The appetiser event is aimed at attracting students on to your course through a fun and entertaining evening that also would include a short evangelistic talk (usually 'Christianity: Boring, Untrue and Irrelevant?') and possibly one or two testimonies.

The evening should be light and accessible to the type of guest that you are hoping to attract on your course. You will therefore need to consider the following advice in light of your situation and the style of evening that you think most suited to your audience.

You can be really creative with the type of event that you plan. We have seen a wide variety of appetisers including jazz funk evenings, celebration suppers, band nights in Students' Unions, 70s fancy dress evenings, small theme dinners in homes and many others.

Try to keep the flavour and size of your appetiser in line with the style and size of your course. For example, if your course will be a small group meeting in a home then a large Students' Union event would not be a realistic way of launching it.

Key elements

Fun

The majority of the event should be non-spiritual and light-hearted. It is a chance to start getting to know the guests and to make them feel welcome and relaxed in a Christian environment.

Basic introduction

The evangelistic talk should be short (maximum 20 minutes) and entertaining, while introducing a gentle challenge for your guests to explore the Christian faith further through the new Alpha for Students course.

Testimony

One or two testimonies are always very effective at an appetiser event. These should be by students who have recently become Christians on Alpha. The best format to use is for a host to ask three simple questions. For this type of testimony it is inadvisable to ask them to prepare much in advance. You should simply run through the following questions with them just before the evening starts and ask them to speak honestly and fairly briefly.

1. Were you a churchgoer ... months ago?
2. What made you decide to attend an Alpha course?
3. What happened?
4. What difference has Jesus made to your life?

Invitation

Your host should offer an open invitation for everyone to come along on the first week of your course. Make sure you have postcard invitations for everyone to take away with them.

The small low-key event

If you are planning a small course, perhaps in your home or room, a low-key appetiser may be perfect as your launch.

You can easily turn a simple idea for your evening into an event that everyone will enjoy and will warm them to the idea of attending the course. Aim either to do something a little different or special, perhaps a theme dinner party or a video evening with a meal – use your imagination to come up with something easy and yet fun. Plan in advance, recruit a little help to make it a team event and advertise it well to your friends' perhaps by creating specific invitations following the theme or activity for your evening.

The larger event

This will involve more work and will definitely need to be a 'team' effort. Here are some basic pointers to help you think through every aspect of the event.

1. Book your venue

Fix your date early and talk to the manager to confirm how you will run your event, how much it will cost and what technical equipment will be provided and what you will need to supply yourself. Other issues to discuss would be catering arrangements, bar or refreshment facilities and health and safety provisions (eg stewarding requirements and costs).

2. Recruit a team

Every good event will need a team of people to work together, so it is essential to delegate specific areas of responsibility to reliable and committed people. These areas may cover things such as promotion, catering, technical, entertainment, follow-up and overall management.

3. Advertising campaign

All successful appetisers rely on people turning up! Plan your advertising schedule to ensure that the event is well publicised in every possible way (*see Chapter 4*).

4. Event content

Plan in advance to ensure you have a speaker and the entertainment or bands that you want. Check that you know all the expenses that this might incur.

5. Prayer

Pray for the success and effectiveness of your appetiser.

6. Finances

You may need to raise some money to help cover the cost of your appetiser mission event. Try to estimate how much the event will cost and seek possible ways of raising it (*see Chapter 1 'Resources: What will you need?'*).

7. Management

Ensure that someone is responsible for pulling everything together throughout the planning stages and overseeing the event itself.

8. Follow-up – your Alpha for Students course

Make sure that your course dates and venue are confirmed and that Alpha Invitations leaflets and *Why Jesus?* booklets are available for all the guests.

Chapter 7

Following the recipe

A typical Alpha session

Although Alpha for Students courses can be very different in style it is helpful to have a basic framework around which to model your course.

The typical Alpha programme would look something like this:

Example – Evening Alpha (with a meal)

6.30pm	*Team prayer meeting*	*To pray, encourage the team, discuss content of the video/talk, answer questions and cover administrative issues.*
7.00pm	**Alpha starts, meal served**	Guests arrive, leaders and helpers are ready to welcome guests and to help them get their meal. Food is eaten in small groups while relationships are built.
7.30pm	**Welcome, joke**	Course leader welcomes guests and tells a joke to put them at ease.
7.40pm	**Worship**	Introduces guests to the practice of corporate worship.
7.45pm	**Video/talk**	Presents guests with information through a factual and well-presented talk. For live speakers you would have a shorter talk (maximum 30 minutes).
8.30pm	**Coffee**	Guests relax over a hot drink and biscuit. Move easily into the discussion group.
8.45pm	**Small group discussion**	Allows guests to discuss in an unthreatening, non-confrontational and accepting environment.
9.30pm	**End**	Group leaders should be prepared to summarise the discussion and close the session promptly.
Après-Alpha	*Time permitting*	*You may want to continue chatting in a more relaxed environment with those who want to go on to somewhere else (whatever would be the most natural activity for your guests).*

You may have to alter your Alpha programme slightly to fit the course into the time you have available, whether or not you are having a meal or refreshments, and the time of day you will hold your sessions. Regardless of your situation it is important to stick to the **Alpha recipe:**

Relationship time (non-spiritual, relax, chat, get to know each other)

Video/talk time (present the information in a suitable manner)

Discussion time (small group time to discuss the talk)

If your plans do not allow you to cover all these areas suitably you should reconsider them and ensure that these vital ingredients are in place.

Chapter 8

Alpha Weekend or Day Away
Introducing the person and work of the Holy Spirit

The weekend away is one of the most important parts of your Alpha for Students course and yet can also be the most frustrating when you run a course specifically for students. However, it is also the most enjoyable and rewarding experience as you begin to see your course come together and make sense.

Why is the weekend so important?

Quite simply for two reasons:

1. Relationships

You have hopefully now realised that there is a huge emphasis in Alpha on building relationships. Taking time out as a group to go away somewhere for a weekend or even a day is a really effective way of cementing these friendships and is often a turning point in the course.

2. Content

The weekend talks explore the third person of the Trinity; the person and work of the Holy Spirit. Guests are given an opportunity to be prayed for, often for the first time. Time and time again God honours simple requests for him to send his Spirit among us. It is only through the work of the Holy Spirit that we are able to see people give their lives to Christ, be filled with the Spirit, get excited about Jesus and subsequently bring their friends on the next course.

A survey carried out by the Methodist Church found a direct correlation between courses that left out the weekend talks and those that were disappointed with their Alpha course.

Which is best – weekend or day away?

A weekend is always the better option. However, if you are unable to plan a whole weekend (Friday – Sunday), you could try to arrive on Saturday morning and stay until Sunday lunchtime. If this were not practical, then taking one day away would be preferable to doing nothing.

Planning

You should schedule the dates for your weekend as soon as you set your course dates. To ensure that all your team can come on your weekend, advise them of the dates as soon as possible and encourage them to enter the dates in their diaries at the earliest opportunity.

Venue

You will now need to find a venue for your weekend.

As you start to search you should consider the following:

1. The estimated size of your course

You will need to find a venue that will be able to accommodate everyone comfortably and aim to keep the same atmosphere as your course, eg if you have a small course it may be a little strange to go away to a huge and impersonal venue.

2. How far do you want to travel?

Try to go somewhere that will not force you to spend the whole weekend travelling. Aim to stay within a couple of hours' travel.

3. How much can your guests afford?

Students notoriously have little or no money and so it is really important to keep the cost as low as possible. You should have a feel for how much might be reasonable for students in your area to pay – we would recommend somewhere between £25 and £50 depending on the type of facilities you aim to have.

4. Where will you look?

- **Friends' houses/personal contacts**

The cheapest and often the nicest place to go, if you are a small course, would be to the home of someone you know. Find out whether any members of your church or friends' parents have a home that they wouldn't mind being taken over for one weekend. This option may be a little cramped but is well worth pursuing.

- **Recommended venues**

Have you, or anyone you know used weekend conference facilities that they would recommend. It is often preferable to go with a personal recommendation as to whether a venue would be suitable for an Alpha weekend.

- **CCI Venue Finder**

Call 0247 655 9099 to advise them of your weekend requirements (UK only). They cannot guarantee to find you somewhere suitable but it is well worth contacting them.

- **Alpha for Students Office**

The UK Alpha for Students Office has a growing file of suitable venues for student weekends away. Let us know your requirements and we will try to help you find a venue. If you are outside the UK please contact your Alpha Office and they might be able to give you some advice.

- **Local churches**

If you are unable to find a venue, or cannot fit in a full weekend, it is a good idea to ask if your local church can help you out or put you in touch with other churches that might have facilities to cater for you on your day away.

Note to remember

The majority of your guests will not yet be Christians, so it is important to make sure that your weekend venue is comfortable, accepting and suitable for all your guests regardless of their spiritual viewpoint.

You may not always be able to visit the proposed venue in advance to check its suitability. Try to discuss the nature of the weekend with the venue people when you confirm the dates to make sure that they know what to expect.

What does it look like?

The key to a great weekend is preparation, to make the weekend smooth, relaxed and easy for your guests.

Live speakers

Even if you have used videos throughout your course, it is always preferable to have live speakers on the weekend away so that your two times of ministry flow more easily. Try to find speakers who are familiar and preferably experienced with the Alpha Holy Spirit material and who will also relate well to the students. If you need help finding suitable local speakers, contact the Alpha for Students Office.

Welcome your guests

It is likely that your guests will never have been on anything like a Christian weekend away before. Since they will inevitably be apprehensive, try to make them feel relaxed and welcome as soon as they arrive.

A few ways to do this would be to:
a) Expect them – have someone there to show them to their room and show them around.
b) Have some chocolates or doughnuts and a drink to help relax them as they settle in.
c) Encourage guests and leaders to travel to the venue together – you may want to co-ordinate travel arrangements or arrange group transport before the weekend to ensure that none of your guests has to travel alone.

Relaxation

As you plan the schedule, ensure that there is plenty of time for guests and team to chill out together and have some fun.

Saturday afternoon – this is a great time to play some sport, go for a walk or some other communal activity.

Saturday evening – chill out after all the sessions for the day. Again a communal activity is preferable but, as long as guests are made to feel at ease and are relaxing together, you can be quite flexible with your plans. For large courses it may be possible to put together some entertainment for the evening, while for smaller courses you may prefer to relax, playing games or something similar. Try putting someone in charge of entertainment for the weekend.

Programme

Whether you have a full weekend or just one day, it is possible to fit all the talks into your allotted time.

See Appendix D for help with programmes for the weekend or day away.

If you need any help planning your weekend please contact the Alpha for Students Office for advice.

Chapter 9

Prayer
Putting it in God's hands

'Evangelism without prayer is like a bomb without a detonator and prayer without evangelism is like a detonator without a bomb.'

Dutch Sheets, *The Prayer Summit*

Prayer is absolutely essential to the success of your course.

Before
Vision meeting
You could arrange a prayer session and invite all the Christians who have a heart for the students in your area or campus. Use it to pray and gather support for the course on every level.

Team training
Following the first two training sessions you could take the time to pray together as a new team. It is also a good time to pray for each other as you embark upon this exciting venture.

During
Pre-Alpha prayer
Use the meeting before your Alpha sessions each week to pray for the relevant aspects of your course.

Leaders and helpers
Encourage the team to pray for each individual in their respective groups. An easy way to do this is to divide the guests between the leaders and helpers and praying for your nominated guests throughout the course.

Before the weekend away
After your team has done the third training session on ministry it is a great time to pray together for the upcoming weekend and for the guests to come along and be touched by God.

Ministry on the weekend
You will have the opportunity to pray directly for your guests on the weekend away. This is a very important part of the course and a real honour for us to pray for God to bless our guests.

In small groups
One of the aims of the small group is to model prayer for your guests. Emphasise to the small group leaders the importance of praying in the group before the week on healing when the groups are encouraged to pray together at the end of the session.

Note – it is always important to use sensitivity in this area. Refer to the team training for more information on how to model prayer.

After
Thank you and please
One idea at the end of your course is to gather people together to thank God for all that he has done throughout course and to ask him to help you as you move on to the next.

Chapter 10
Worship

Introducing your guests to worship through songs

If possible, it is preferable to have worship on your Alpha for Students course from Week 1. This is a key part of the course and, although often difficult for new guests, it frequently becomes a highlight by the end of the course.

> **It is important to remember that your guests will have little or no experience of Christian worship. We recommend that you follow these guidelines for worship throughout the course, being sensitive to your guests as they grow in their relationship with God.**

When to sing?

- Worship immediately before the talk or video.

- Sing just two songs at the beginning of the course and build up to four or five by the end of the course (mainly after the weekend away).

What to sing?

- Use songs that express objective truths rather than belief in or love for God (these can be introduced later on).

- Mix some familiar traditional hymns with contemporary worship, which will probably be totally new to your guests.

- Be careful to build familiarity with songs by repeatedly using those that are new or less known.

See Appendix F for a 'Suggested song list' to help you select your worship.

Things to remember

- If the singing isn't too loud – don't worry! Truth is being sung.

- There is plenty of time for your guests to get used to worship.

- Don't pressure them to participate and be patient.

- Help your guests to relax by encouraging them to do whatever they wish, eg 'Please sit or stand and join in if you want to.'

- Moderate your normally fervent worship and encourage your team to do the same, eg worshipping in a way that does not threaten your guests or make them feel uncomfortable. Participate in the style that you would hope them to worship – make it easy for them to join in. However, enjoy the worship by singing loudly, smiling and showing that this is pleasant!

- Your worship leader should keep their eyes open to help them connect with the group – smile and relax.

- Hold back from interjecting between songs with prayers and mini-sermons. Just let the worship flow.

- Ensure that you plan in advance which songs you will sing, in which order, and that you have the necessary overhead transparencies or song sheets available and ready to go.

- PRAY!

Note – Very small groups with less than 12 people may find it hard to include worship on their course. There is really no way round this problem; however, it is preferable to have worship of some kind during your weekend or day away if at all possible.

Chapter 11

After it's all over

A new beginning?

As your course reaches its conclusion we hope you will be looking at a very different group of guests from when you started. The main aim of running an Alpha course is to bring people into a relationship with God and subsequently to send each person from the course into an environment where they will grow and enjoy their new life as a Christian.

Follow-up

If your course is just for students, you may not have the opportunity to encourage your guests into a church environment that is already known to them and that they are comfortable with. It is therefore worth considering what is available to your students and where you might encourage them to get involved.

Church

It is vital for all Christians, both new and old, to be involved with their local church. Alpha may be the first Christian environment that your guests have freely entered into and it will very quickly become the 'norm' for their spiritual activity.

Introducing your guests to church can often be a big challenge. One way of easing them into this environment would be to invite everyone to come to church after travelling back from your weekend away. If your team attend a variety of churches, you could suggest that guests go along with their own group leaders, helpers or friends (for evening services). If your churches only hold morning services or if you are holding a day away, you could encourage your team to invite their friends to church during the last few weeks of the course (sensitivity will be needed

when doing this). From this they can be encouraged by their new friends to get involved in the life of the church they choose to settle in.

Christian Union and other student groups

As students, your guests will probably be in a privileged position to be able to get involved with other Christian groups in addition to being part of a church.

Relationships are probably the highest influencing factor here, because guests will generally choose to join in with Christian activity on campus with people they already know.

It is important that, while encouraging your guests into a environment where they might flourish, you should not pressure them to join any specific groups or even to join in with everything that is happening. The key would be to invite them along and make sure they know they are welcome without feeling obligated.

Creating your next team

Guests who have recently become Christians are perfect to join the team for your next Alpha course. They are excited about their new relationship with God, filled with the Holy Spirit and yet undoubtedly are still surrounded by their non-Christian friends who will be starting to realise that something has happened to them.

End of course celebration

Your guests will usually be keen to invite their friends along to an end of course celebration event. It will give them an opportunity to explain what they have been doing throughout the course, introduce old friends to new ones and bring them into an environment where they will be encouraged to come on the next course.

Picking your team

Ask your current leaders to recommend any of their guests who they think might be perfect to help on your next team. They don't need to be spiritually mature or to be a great theologian in order to be on the team and it is usually possible to find a role for anyone who wants to join in.

One thing to consider when inviting new Christians to help in your small groups might be to try and put them with a group leader who is more experienced and mature in their faith. After they have helped on one course, and have seen Alpha from the team perspective, they will most likely be well prepared to lead a group the next time round.

Encouraging your guests to be on your team is a fantastic way of encouraging their growth as new Christians.

Still not a Christian?

We are increasingly seeing people arrive on Alpha from further and further back in their spiritual journeys. It is therefore probable that you will have some guests who want to continue to meet together as a group and yet have not made the step to become Christians.

Within the context of the local church, a Christian group on campus or just some friends getting together, you may want to consider running a follow-up group to address guests' specific issues wherever they are at.

Alpha materials that might be for useful for small group study are:

- *Searching Issues*
- *Questions of Life*
- *A Life Worth Living*
- *Challenging Lifestyle*

Additionally you may like to recommend *30 Days* as an aid for individual study.

See Appendix B for recommended follow-up material.

Chapter 12

Talk alternatives

Getting the truth across

As you plan your course consider how you want to convey the content to your guests. You have several options:

Watch the videos

Alpha for Students use the same videos as mainstream Alpha courses. These are available in box sets comprising the entire course or you can buy individual tapes that contain three talks on each one. An Alpha video session is a talk of approximately 45 minutes and is presented by the Revd Nicky Gumbel.

Invite outside speakers

You could invite speakers to do the talks. You may know people from local churches or suitable Christian organisations who you could ask. Alternatively, you could contact the Alpha for Students Office to enquire about Alpha Advisors or other recommended speakers in your area. Ensure that guest speakers are suitable, ie that they are able to relate to a student audience and that they are already very familiar with the Alpha material.

Do the talks yourself

The Alpha course material is presented in a logical and accessible way to make it easily reproduced. If you have individuals on your team who are either used to public speaking or who are keen to be challenged in that area, this would be a perfect opportunity to use their skills.

- **See 'talk structure' in the Alpha manual**
You will need to follow the points in the manual. This will help you plan the framework of your talk.

- **Read *Questions of Life***
Each talk has a coinciding chapter and is very helpful when looking in depth at the content to be included.

- **Watch the video / listen to the audio of the talk**
Many people find it helpful to do this to understand fully the flow and emphasis of the talk.

- **Vary the length of the talk**
If you do the talks yourself you will be able to reduce their length to fit the timing of your Alpha sessions. You may need to cover certain points in less detail.

- **Apply your own illustrations**
You should feel free to change the illustrations and stories if the ones given are not applicable or if you have personal examples that would help explain your point.

Both live speakers and video

You may choose to use a combination of live speakers and video. As you decide what to do you should consider the following:

When it is preferable to use videos	When it is preferable to use live speakers
• *Groups of less than 12* • *When you have no suitable live speakers* • *When you have deaf guests (videos with subtitles are available)*	• *Groups of more than 40* • *Weekend away talks 'How Can I Be Filled With the Spirit?' and 'How Can I Make the Most of the Rest of My Life?'* • *'Does God Heal Today?'* • *When combining two talks (see below)*

5. Combining two talks

This may be necessary if you are trying to fit your Alpha for Students course into a shorter term (*see Appendix C*). You can either ask a guest speaker to do this or attempt to do it yourself. Follow the same guidelines as point three above. You will need to reduce the material considerably to fit the combined talks into a suitable timeslot. A combined talk should be no longer than 45 minutes (preferably 30 minutes).

Recommended talk combinations are as follows:

- *Why and How Should I Read the Bible?* and *Why and How Should I Pray?*

- *Who Is the Holy Spirit?* and *What Does the Holy Spirit Do?*

- *Why and How Should We Tell Others?* and *Does God Heal Today?*

- *Why and How Should We Tell Others?* and *What About the Church?*

Talks that we recommend you **do not** combine with any others are:

- *Christianity: Boring, Untrue and Irrelevant?*

- *Who Is Jesus?*

- *Why Did Jesus Die?*

- *How Can I Be Sure of My Faith?*

- *How Can I Be Filled With the Spirit?*

- *How Can I Resist Evil?*

Note – **It is advisable only to combine talks when you really have to.** It is always preferable to have just one talk and topic per Alpha session.

Chapter 13

Alpha as a follow-up to mission

Catching the interested

Alpha is a perfect tool to be used as a follow-up course after a mission event or week that runs either on or off campus.

Alpha for Students is being used effectively in many universities to work with those students who have visited guest lectures or events and have expressed an interest in exploring the Christian faith in more depth.

If you are planning a mission event(s) it is worth considering the following points as you prepare for your follow-up Alpha for Students course.

Logistics and preparation

Your mission will undoubtedly provide you with a great deal of work. It would therefore be good to nominate another person to be the administrator of your Alpha for Students course if it will be too much to cover the planning for both effectively. Your new administrator will be responsible for arranging every aspect of the course and delegating if necessary.

Complete as much as possible of your preparation BEFORE your mission week starts. You will need to have all the relevant information available at the start of the mission to advertise your course effectively to every guest.

Key things to have completed BEFORE mission week:

> *Team appointed   *Advertising commenced
> *Venue confirmed   *Team trained
> *Dates and time confirmed *Weekend/day booked

See Chapters 1–6 for step by step advice on how to get the course organised and started.

Advertising

Although your events will offer you the opportunity to announce your course, it is essential that you advertise your course more widely. Ensure the following areas are covered:

Invitations

Have an abundance of invitations available at all of your events. Give one to every person who attends as a reminder of the verbal announcement.

Announcement

Have someone announce the details of the course at a suitable point at every event.

Posters

As with any Alpha course, your posters will serve as a back up reminder to those around campus that the course is starting near them soon.

Testimonies

One or two testimonies from students who have recently become Christians on Alpha would be very effective in a mission event (*see testimony guidelines in Chapter 6*).

Personal invitation

Again the most important method of advertising your course is to encourage all the Christians you know to invite all their friends on the course regardless of whether they attended the mission events or not.

Other

See Chapter 4 for more suggestions about how you might advertise your course.

Course timing

You will probably encounter difficulties if you are trying to squeeze your course into one academic term following a pre-arranged mission.

If at all possible, still endeavour to run the course without a break. However, if you are faced with less than seven weeks, consider finishing the course the following term or semester.

See Chapters 1–2 and Appendix C for more detailed help on scheduling your course. For more specific advice on working around obstacles, contact the Alpha for Students Office.

Mission content

Christianity: Boring, Untrue and Irrelevant?

Most Alpha for Students courses start with an appetiser event to attract people on the new course. The evangelistic message usually used for these events is the talk *Christianity: Boring, Untrue and Irrelevant?* This talk is often accompanied by one or two testimonies from individuals who have recently come to faith in Christ (preferably as a result of attending an Alpha course) which serve as an encouragement and taster to potential guests.

See Chapter 6 for more help on how to run a mission style appetiser event.

Chapter 14

Alpha for Students in the local church

Drawing students into the local Christian community

Since Alpha for Students was established in 1998 we have seen the course be very successful in the context of the local church.

Many churches have universities and colleges in their area and often feel unprepared and without the skills needed to reach out into a culture so different from their own. Alpha for Students is a tool that can be effective for local churches to welcome young people into their communities. It provides them with a culturally relevant and accessible course through which their guests can discover for themselves more about the Christian faith.

Churches that already run regular Alpha have found that adapting their courses in the following ways has encouraged students to attend and has allowed them to run Alpha for Students as part of their normal Alpha course.

What is essential when reaching out to students?
There are three things which you should pay particular to attention as you plan to run Alpha for Students at your church:

1. Groups *for* students *led by* students

Students will talk about different things in a different way to most of the other guests on your Alpha course. To ensure that you make provision for their needs, keep at least one group dedicated to student-age guests led by students.

If you have no students in your church reconsider how you might attract them on to your course. Start by reading Chapter 1 'Who will be on your team?' and contact all the Christian groups that are active on campus. Work with these people to try and gain support to help on your course and to draw fellow students in.

2. Run your course to fit academic terms/semesters

It is likely that the majority of students in your area will come from other parts of the country. As you plan for the course it would be advisable to contact the universities and colleges in your vicinity to ask for their term dates. It is important to plan your course around these dates to make it as easy as possible for students to attend. If your guests are forced to miss either the beginning or end of the course it is less likely that they will come along at all. It is possible that you may have to reduce the length of your course in order to fit it in.

3. Advertise on campus

The best place to find students is on campus at your local university or college. You will need your students to assist you in gaining permission or access to display posters on campus.

• *It is important to remember that advertising alone is not sufficient to get students on your course.* **The best people to reach students are students.** *Recruit the help of your church students, their friends and Christian colleagues to invite their friends on to the course. Personal invitation is the most effective way of getting people on your course and without this being encouraged it is unlikely that your course will attract very many students.*

Chapter 15

Getting creative
Playing with the packaging

The gospel is a message that we need never attempt to change, nor should we ever try. However, the packaging through which we present the gospel is a medium that we are responsible for. We can do everything within our power to make our Alpha for Students course as culturally relevant and accessible as possible.

There is no fixed or correct method of making Alpha for Students culturally relevant. Every course will attract a different group of students and hence you will need to decide which is the best way of adapting your course in order to suit your guests.

Below are a few ideas and suggestions to help you start thinking in the right direction.

Atmosphere

As previously discussed, you can be really creative when you choose your venue. Try to find a great place where your course will be most effective in attracting and keeping guests. Alternatively, think of ways to turn even the most normal or 'churchy' of rooms into a friendly, atmospheric and comfortable place. This would apply to your regular weekly room, your appetiser venue and your weekend accommodation.

See Chapter 6 for more ideas on how to be creative with your appetiser event.

You could try adding simple things like:
- Tea light candles
- Avoid theatre style set up

- Place tables and chairs in relaxed format
- Muted lighting
- Background music (non-Christian)
- Throws
- Curtains or coloured tissue paper over bare windows
- Table coverings
- Having sweets or chocolates scattered in bowls

Talks

If you choose live speakers you have the option to be creative with your presentation. There is no one 'right' way of doing this. We would encourage you to think broadly of film clips, song lyrics, brief poems, excerpts from books or even paintings that you think would help to emphasise a point or explain it more clearly. Be careful not to overindulge your own interests. For example, be aware that not everyone in your audience may have the same passion for poetry or art as you. However, do try to explore using these alternative illustrations, because they will keep your talks fresh and relevant.

Key things to remember when using your creativity:
- Don't use too many examples or include them for the sake of it.

- Only use the illustration if it genuinely help emphasise the point.

- Put yourself in the shoes of your guest – they may not share your expertise or passion – will they get it?

- Ensure that any excerpts you use would be within Christian moral boundaries.

- Whatever you use, make sure that it is culturally

relevant to your audience – 21ˢᵗ century student culture moves very quickly.

- Be careful not to patronise your guests.

Copyright: The law is confusing over the use of specific video clips. Film and video companies have advised that technically it is illegal to show all or part of a hired film to anyone other than your family. However, in practice the law is extremely difficult to interpret. As no one has ever been taken to court over this issue, there is no established precedent. Normally, distribution companies do not mind clips of their films being shown as long as:

- It is only a tiny part of the whole film
- No money is changing hands
- No profit is being made

Things NOT to change

We would encourage you to be creative with as many elements of Alpha for Students as possible. However, there are some essential components of the course that we would recommend that you use, since they stick to the Alpha recipe.

- **Talk content and structure**
While personalising the talks and making them your own with illustrations and creatives, be careful to stick to the structure presented in the *Alpha manual* and *Questions of Life*. You may want to trim certain parts down, especially if you are limited for time, but do not compromise the overall content of the message.

- **Alpha manuals**
It is always preferable to use the manuals – give one to each guest to keep.

- **Why Jesus?**
As guests on your course choose to begin relationships with God it is essential to have these booklets available.

- **Training**
The content of the Alpha training should always be completely covered whether you use the videos or live speakers. It is during the training that the principles of Alpha are communicated to your team and they are equipped with practical guidelines of how to lead on Alpha. The training can be the making or breaking of your Alpha for Students course. It is vital to include it.

- **Overall session style**
The overall format of Alpha should always be the same to maintain the balance of ingredients. These essential elements are:

  – A relaxed, informal and non-spiritual period (preferably over food or refreshments)

  – Talk or video

  – Small group discussion

- **Overall content of the course**
All the main topics covered in Alpha should always be included. It is permissible to omit or combine one or two of the latter talks but is vital that certain areas are not missed out (*please see page 96 for copyright details*).

Chapter 16

Giving your course a health check

Is it as good as it gets?

Alpha for Students is designed to work effectively as part of a rolling programme. This means that one course is ideally followed by another on the subsequent term or semester and then again and again.

To avoid repeating the same mistakes, and to give your course a health check, consider the following areas after each course to ensure that everything is working to make your course as good as it can possibly be.

Identifying weak areas

If your answer is no to any of the following questions, please see the page number listed for advice on that area.

		If no, see page

Advertising

• Is your course registered on the Alpha Course Directory?	☐	16
• Do you advertise on campus?	☐	26–29
• Did you explore alternative creative ways to advertise your course?	☐	26–29
• Did many students PERSONALLY invite their friends to come along?	☐	26
• Did you launch your course with an appetiser event?	☐	33

Timing

• Does your course run within the term time of your local university or college?	☐	13
• Is your weekly meeting at a convenient time for the majority of students you are trying to reach?	☐	13
• Did you run your course within just one term?	☐	14
• Did your Alpha sessions always run according to schedule (ie everything starting and finishing on time)?	☐	35

Venue

• Was your venue on or near the campus?	☐	13
• Was your venue easy to find (did you use directional signs)?	☐	13
• Was your venue friendly and welcoming to non-church going students?	☐	13

Team

If no,
see page

- Did **you invite** the people you wanted to be your group leaders and helpers? ☐ 17
- Did all your leaders and helpers do **all three** Alpha training sessions? ☐ 30–32
- Did you hold a prayer and administration meeting before each weekly session? ☐ 23
- Did your team attend every week including the weekend or day away? ☐ 17

Logistics

- Did you cover all three components of the relaxed non-spiritual time, talk and small group discussion? ☐ 49
- Did you provide food or refreshments at the beginning of the session? ☐ 12, 24
- Did you provide drinks after the talk to lead into the small group discussion time? ☐ 25
- Was your room set up and ready when your guests arrived each week? ☐ 18, 23
- Was an Alpha manual given to each guest at the first session they attended? ☐ 24
- Were name labels given to everyone during the first three weeks? ☐ 24
- Did you have Bibles available for your guests? ☐ 24
- Did you have any of the recommended books available for sale or distribution? ☐ 25
- Did you have sufficient money to cover all your expenses? ☐ 54
- Did you have worship from Week 1? ☐ 40, 84
- Did you use questionnaires at the end of the course? ☐ 21, 85
- Did you have one person responsible for pulling all the arrangements together for your course? ☐ 15
- If your course had more than one small group, did you have people to greet new guests during the first two weeks? ☐ 23

Weekend away

- Did you go away for a weekend? ☐ 36-38
- Did you invite your guests and provide them with full details at least three weeks before? ☐ 20-21
- Were all your guests able to afford to go to the weekend away? ☐ 21, 54
- Did you have worship during your weekend away? ☐ 40, 84

- Did you change/add/omit any of the recommended weekend talks? ☐ 36-38, 96

- Did you have prayer ministry during the weekend away? ☐ 30-31, 36, 39

- Did you have time to relax together as a group over the weekend, eg go for a walk together, play sport or games? ☐ 38, 78-80

- If you ran your course over two terms, did you fit your weekend in before the break? ☐ 20, 72-77

Small groups

- Did your small group times remain true to the principles and practical guidelines explained in the training sessions? ☐ 31

- Did you have less than 10 guests per small group? ☐ 19-20

- Were the majority of your guests already Christians? ☐ 19-20

- Had many guests in your small groups previously done Alpha? ☐ 19-20

- Did more than 70 per cent of your guests keep attending throughout the course? ☐ 30-32

- Did you find it easy to transfer guests from your small groups into church Community life? ☐ 41-42

Talks

- If you had live speakers, did your talks ever run over 30 minutes? ☐ 43-44

- If you used the videos, were you happy with the style, form and content? ☐ 43

- If you did the talks yourself, did you feel that they were of a high enough standard? ☐ 43

- Did you miss out or fundamentally change any of the talks? ☐ 43-44, 72-77, 96

- If you had live speakers, did they stick to the order and content of the talks (as in the manual)? ☐ 43-44

Preventing burnout

In our experience, team burnout is the most common reason for an Alpha for Students course to dwindle and then eventually finish.

The key to keeping yourself and your team fresh is to have a healthy turnover of people. As your guests become Christians, get excited about God and get filled with the Holy Spirit, encourage them to help lead on the next course in any way they can. As these very enthusiastic people help you, they will inevitably bring their friends along as guests and so the cycle continues. This means that you and others can take a break for a course or two and then come back to Alpha envisioned and refreshed. The alternative would be always using the same team and leadership who are tired and possibly disillusioned as they come to a stalemate with no new team or guests coming on the course.

As a course administrator, always have in mind someone to work closely with you, who would be able to take over the running of the course when you need a well-deserved break.

Chapter 17

Financing your course
Knocking on the right doors

Depending upon the size, venue and style of the course, running Alpha for Students can vary in expense quite considerably.

Predict your budget

As you plan your course, predict realistically how large or small you anticipate your course to be and then draw up a budget for the known or anticipated costs you might incur. Use the following as a guide:

Predicted budget	
Venue hire for entire course	£
Cost of catering less any food donations expected	£
Alpha manuals *(one per guest)*	£
Alpha videos *(if needed)*	£
Alpha training videos and manuals *(one per guest)*	£
Weekend expenses *(not covered by income received)*	£
Advertising expenses (including posters, invitations, printing and other resources used)	£
Estimated cost for Alpha for Students course	**£**

Raise the money

Once you have estimated how much money you will need for your course, you could use some or all of the following people to raise money to support your course.

- **Your team** – Give your team the opportunity to give some of their own money.

- **Christian Union, chaplaincy or other campus group or society** – Some groups have a budget for evangelism – they might like to give some of it towards your course.

- **Local churches** – You could ask churches in your area if they would like to sponsor the course.

Or you could:

- **Take an offering** – This is great on your weekend away after the last talk and ministry. God has frequently provided in this way to cover expenses for the weekend and course.

- **Sponsor a student** – Ask any of the above whether they would like to provide money to put one student through the course, including the weekend or day away. They can also commit to pray for the person(s) throughout the course.

- **Fund-raising evening** – You could run a fun event to raise funds.

Chapter 18

Case studies

What is it really like?

Gemma Murphy is a student and has been involved in running Alpha for Students at Trinity College Dublin.

Who is responsible for running your course?

The Christian Union (CU) – I have been the course administrator and have a team of seven others. Six of us have been group leaders/helpers; one gave the talks and one led the worship.

What type of venue do you use for your Alpha for Students sessions?

A room in college that is quite big but still cosy. It has a kitchen attached to it so that we can make tea, coffee etc.

What format does your average session take?

At 6.30pm everyone arrives and mingles. We always have tea, coffee, drinks, biscuits etc.

We usually start at 7pm – we sing a few songs and then have the talk. After the talk we have a short tea/coffee break and then go into our discussion groups for about 45 minutes to one hour.

Do you provide a meal or refreshments?

We didn't have the funds to prepare a meal every week but on one occasion we had a pizza night, on another night (Pancake Tuesday) we made pancakes and got people to bring in whatever topping they wanted.

One night, a couple of the guests decided to make Banoffee Pie for everyone and as the course went on guests started to bring biscuits, cookies, doughnuts, chocolate etc of their own accord for everyone to share. I think it is so important to have some sort of food and drink every week because it helps people to relax and get to know each other.

What support or input have you had from other student organisations or churches?

The CU ran Alpha but it really became a separate course that ran itself but the CU did commit to pray for it and for every Alpha supper they brought desserts. There were various churches that prayed for us and helped us financially.

Can you describe what happened from hearing about Alpha for Students until the point where you had your course ready to start?

We began to think about people that we thought would be particularly good in an Alpha group situation and nearly everyone who we asked was very positive. A number of new people in the CU stood out and we approached them and asked them if they would like to be involved. Our IFES relay worker also showed a real interest. It turned out that the group leaders and helpers offered experience from a wide variety of backgrounds.

I think it helps to have people who have a good knowledge of the basics of Christianity themselves and also people who have a real heart for sharing the gospel with people in a friendly, non-confrontational kind of way. Those of us who could made preparations for going to the Alpha conference, which we found very helpful and it answered a lot of our questions. We purchased resources *(Questions of Life, Searching Issues, Why Jesus?* Alpha manuals, training manuals, a worship pack and drink mats) using our student discount, which was so helpful!

When college began in October we all got together to begin praying and planning for Alpha and trying to organise the schedule. We decided to start it in our second term, which would give us enough time to plan and publicise properly. During the first term we really encouraged the CU members to pray for Alpha and to be thinking and praying about friends who they'd like to ask to come to the Alpha supper. We had our Alpha supper in November towards the end of term and on the basis of the numbers of people that signed up we began to plan for and book our venue for the weekend away.

How did you prepare your team for the course?
Some of us were able to go to the conference and this was invaluable! We shared what we learnt with the rest of the team and followed the training manual for the various training sessions to prepare us for the course. We spent a lot of time praying for the people who had signed up and for each other.

How did you launch your course – did you run an appetiser event?
We had an Alpha Supper in November, just before we finished for our Christmas holidays. Weeks before, we encouraged the CU to pray for their non-Christian friends and to write down the names of three to five of those friends who they would like to invite to the Alpha Supper. We printed invitations, which we encouraged them to take and give to those friends, and we blitzed the campus with invitations, posters and fliers. We put the drinks mats in the two bars in college and set up information stands in the two main buildings in college where people could come and take info about the Alpha course and be invited to the supper.

The Supper itself was a great success. We held it in the room where we were planning to run the course and we decorated the room with fairy lights, throws, cushions, flowers, and candles. We set out a huge banquet table in the middle of the room and had loads of finger food! Then we had a short presentation about the course that consisted of *What is Alpha? Who is it for? When is it? Why Alpha?* We showed a short video clip from *Jerry Maguire* to finish our presentation and then encouraged people to sign up if they wanted.

We really emphasised that although it was a long course they could come and go as they pleased and we didn't put any pressure on them to make huge commitments to it. We then brought out the dessert and had tea, coffee and hot chocolate. There was a really nice atmosphere. We wanted to make it as relaxed and friendly as possible and I think it paid off – people didn't seem to want to leave! A lot of people commented particularly on the friendly, warm atmosphere and it was even nominated for 'Best Event of the Year' a couple of weeks ago.

Describe your first Alpha session.
The team met to pray before the evening started. It was quite stressful because we had no concrete idea of how many people would turn up and how they would react to the talks. Therefore we could only provisionally work out the groups because a) people might turn up who hadn't signed up and b) people who had signed up might not turn up. So we had to be totally flexible. On the basis of those already signed up, we slotted people into one of the three discussion groups and when any new people came in who hadn't signed up we got them to fill in their details on a sheet and slotted them in one of the groups.

We had a table where people could come and get a name badge and an Alpha manual and find out what discussion group they would be in.

We had lots of tea, coffee and biscuits and encouraged people to chat and get to know each other. We had our welcome and introduction and explained the format of the night. We didn't have any worship on the first night. I think we were conscious that we didn't want to frighten them all off or make them feel as if they were at church. We wanted to keep it as informal and light as possible.

We had our first talk and then we split into our three groups. We had a break to get more refreshments before the group discussions started. In each of the groups we played a couple of ice-breaker games to try and get to know people a bit better and then began to discuss what we thought of the talk.

In my own group we asked them if they had any questions or issues in particular that they would like us to try and deal with at some point during the course and we wrote them all down in a list. We explained that we would not get them all answered on the first night but that we would deal with all of the issues in some way throughout the course.

How many people came on your course?

We had between 12 and 27 throughout the whole course and it varied every week but there was a core group of people who came most weeks – the majority of them were not Christians. They were mostly undergraduates but there was one mature student and one post-grad and a few international students who were just in Trinity for a year. The group was very varied with people from different faiths, traditions and backgrounds and it was really interesting to hear everyone's beliefs and opinions.

What happened on your weekend or day away?

We went for the weekend down to Avoca Manor in Co. Wicklow. It was very low key, friendly and informal. On the Friday night we had a meal together (we decorated the table with candles and we had music to create a nice cosy atmosphere) and then

briefly chatted about the format for the weekend, washed the dishes and watched videos and chatted.

On Saturday we did three talks (we had an outside speaker who is actually a lecturer in college and has had a lot of experience with Alpha in his own church) and in between we ate lots of food and had some free time down in Avoca village. On Saturday night the speaker gave people the opportunity to receive Jesus and be filled with the Holy Spirit. Although the evening was very low key it was clear that God was moving and that real transformation was going on. On Sunday morning we had our final talk (by the Alpha team) and we spent a bit of time giving our own testimonies of what God meant to us.

The weekend was really great and we got to know each other so well. We took a video camera and did some mini-interviews. Everyone said that they would never forget the weekend and that they had benefited so much from doing the course. A number of them shared how their experience of Jesus had changed and that they felt different.

Did you see any difference in your course when you returned from your weekend away?

Definitely – you could sense that there was a lot more freedom and the people who had gone on the weekend were more at ease and felt more comfortable sharing and discussing things.

Did you run any type of celebration event at the end of your course to lead into the next one?

We had another Alpha Supper so that those who had done the course could invite their friends to hear what it was all about. For this Alpha Supper I asked a few people who had done the course to share a bit about their experience. I asked them three questions: *Why did you do Alpha? How did you benefit from doing the course?* and *Would you recommend it to others?* The team was totally overwhelmed by the responses that were given about how God had impacted their lives through Alpha and amazed to discover that some of the most unlikely people had become Christians as a result of the Alpha course.

Is there anything you would like to tell us?

Alpha for Students does work! It might not be perfect but it is a great tool for evangelism and an effective way to reach out to students in university. I think the key is to make it as relaxed, friendly and informal as possible – many of the students who did Alpha in Trinity College said that that was what they enjoyed most about Alpha. We didn't put pressure on people to come every week or to believe a certain thing. We gave them time to discover things for themselves and to make up their own minds (that way people will keep coming back for more).

Some students became Christians and some didn't but all of them benefited in some way from doing the course and who knows in what way God has been working in their hearts. We don't save people – God does. We just have to be the seed sowers and, for me, that's what Alpha is all about...planting seeds. It's really important to set up some sort of follow-up group to Alpha. After all, Jesus didn't say, 'Go out and get people saved.' He said, 'Go and make disciples.'

Although it is necessary to keep the Alpha content as it is, it is possible to adapt the way you do the course depending on what suits your circumstances. I think it's helpful to keep evaluating how the course is going and to look for ways of improving it. This was our first Alpha course and we were really pleased with how it went but I'm sure that some changes will be made for the next

course and that we will have to keep looking for new and better ways of running the course each year.

Philip Thomas is the Student Pastor at Woodlands Christian Centre in Bristol and the Assistant Chaplain at Bristol University. He has led an Alpha for Students course at his church.

What type of venue do you use?

Church hall. We have once used a student flat in a hall of residence.

What format does your average session take?

Meal (something easy to prepare like pasta, curry or pizza), then a short talk (20 minutes maximum), then small groups.

What support have you had from other student groups or churches?

We have done one Alpha course in partnership with the Christian Union, which was held in a student's flat. For our other courses we have informed the CU but we have run them by ourselves.

How many times have you run Alpha for Students and when did you start?

Started about 1999, and we have done it five or six times.

Can you describe what happened from hearing about Alpha for Students until the point where you had your course ready to start?

I recruited students who I thought would be suitable helpers and then used them, their friends or recent converts to help on subsequent courses.

How did you advertise your course?

Fliers, posters, balloons, invitations etc.

Is there anything you would like to tell us?

I think that brevity is the key for the talks, and a venue near a pub so that people can move on there after the small group time.

Josie Dunlop is a Student Pastor at King's Community Church in Wolverhampton and a recent graduate of the University of Wolverhampton. She has administrated two Alpha for Students courses at her old university, the most recent ran on campus in the Students' Union bar.

Who is responsible for running your course?

I put together a Alpha core team that consisted of the Christian Union committee and local church representatives (from churches where the church had students attending). The core team met once a month throughout the course to pray, give feedback and be updated on how things were going. We also had a review meeting once the course had finished where we were able to give a financial breakdown of the total running costs and feed back on the good and the bad. Consideration was also given to how we could keep the momentum going and how we could continue to work with local church support.

What type of venue do you use for your Alpha for Students sessions?

We met in the Students' Union bar and used their big screen projector for the videos.

What format does your average session take?

6pm	– set up
6.30 – 7pm	– small group leaders and helpers prayer meeting
7.30pm	– food is served
8pm	– welcome, joke
8.10pm	– start videos
9pm	– toilet, drinks break and small groups
9.45pm	– finish

Do you provide a meal or refreshments – if so, what type and how do you prepare it?

A free meal was provided but no drinks because the bar was open for people to get their own. Due to university policy we were unable to do our own catering and had to use the university catering for all the food. It worked well as there was no preparation or washing up to be done. The only down side was that it was very expensive, but because the venue was the main consideration we decided to go ahead with it.

What support have you had from other student organisations or churches?

Local churches (mostly those that students were already attending) were approached by me prior to the course commencing and talked through the vision for the Alpha course. They were invited to help in three ways – the first was with financial support, the second was practical support (cooking and serving, which was later not needed) and thirdly prayer support. In total we received £1237 from the local churches. At an all night prayer meeting for the Black Country, with over 1500 people attending, we announced the Alpha course was running and time was given to praying for the event. I know that prayer groups throughout the city added us to their priorities.

The course was run through the Christian society at the university. This made it possible for it to be held on university property. It also meant that the room was free of charge and the free photocopying facilities that societies get was useful for the publicity.

Further into the course, we set up a sponsor a student scheme, which allowed individuals in local churches to sponsor a student to go on the Holy Spirit weekend away. They were invited to contribute £15 to help subsidise the £25 cost of the weekend. The total received from this was £380.

How many times have you run Alpha for Students and when did you start?

This is the second time I have run a course. The first was in October 2001 – I ran this course from my home with the students and young adults from my church. It was supported and funded by my church and three ladies from church did the cooking each week.

Where did you first hear about Alpha for Students – and how did this encourage you to run a course yourself?

I was invited to come to the Alpha for Students Conference in September 2001 by a student worker friend of mine. At that point I had never run a course, never even been on one, but had only heard good things about them. My main reason for going was to spend some time with my friend. However, at the conference I was challenged, inspired and provoked. I heard how some courses were being run in pubs and homes and thought to myself, 'I could do that.' Three weeks later I started the first course from my home.

Can you describe what happened from hearing about Alpha for Students until the point where you had your course ready to start?

I must have read my vision statement out so many times, to all the local church pastors, the CU committee, the CU, the Students' Union executive and anyone else who would listen. With the backing of my pastor, I arranged a meeting with the CU committee. This is where I presented the idea of running Alpha in the Students' Union. At that time it was quite controversial because it was proposing that the normal CU meetings would be replaced for a period of 10 weeks by the Alpha course. The venue would not be hidden away, it was somewhere very public. It would challenge everything the CU had ever done before.

Then there was the challenge of how to set everything in motion. I left it with the committee for two weeks to decide and talk things through; they came back to me within a week with a unanimous yes. An evening was set aside to present the proposal to the CU. The committee and I answered any questions and concerns and then a vote was taken and it was a unanimous yes. We then began to get local support and build the core team. The rest is history! From the initial proposal to the beginning of the course was about four and a half months.

How did you prepare your team for the course?

The Alpha for Students team came to lead our training one evening and trained the whole of the CU on leading small groups and pastoral care. This was an extremely useful night and people began to get very excited.

Even if they weren't going to be a small group leader or helper it gave people an understanding of what Alpha was about and who it was for. I would recommend being trained this way rather than the video because it was the question and answer time at the end that was the best.

Another night was allocated to publicity and distribution. The evening was spent with everyone from the CU sticking labels onto flyers, overprints onto posters and then being allocated an area or a building to distribute the publicity. These two nights helped create a sense of ownership of the course. We also set aside a couple of nights of prayer specifically for the Alpha course and praying for the people we were going to invite.

How did you launch your course – did you run an appetiser event?

We called it the 'Alpha launch night' and held it in the bar where the course would run. On the days leading up to the launch, fliers were handed out in the Students' Union corridors. We had a band, a buffet and a live talk – 'Christianity; Boring, Untrue and Irrelevant?' There were 80 people that night.

How did you advertise your course?

We used the Alpha for Students publicity (posters, postcards and beer mats) and distributed them across campus (and in halls of residence); there was also a half page newspaper article in the university paper. We worked with Agape (Christian Student Action) from Birmingham and had a night of evangelism training followed the next day by taking questionnaires in the university and talking to people. The questionnaires gave us an opportunity to talk to people to invite them to the Alpha course.

How many people came on your course?

There were 102 names on the register and on average there were 45 people each week.

What happened on your weekend or day away?

Unfortunately, the weekend away fell on Mothering Sunday and many of the students went home for the weekend. Twenty people came on the weekend. It was great fun; we played lots of mad games and had some excellent teaching. We had a speaker rather than the videos.

Did you see any difference in your course when you returned from your weekend away?

The weekend built much stronger friendships between those who went on it and that really shows even now the course has finished.

Is there anything you would like to tell us?

The friendships have been the key. People did come from seeing the posters but those who stayed were those who were invited or brought by a friend and felt they belonged. God has been so faithful throughout.

Vicki Walker is a student at the University of Surrey in Roehampton. After making a re-commitment on an Alpha for Students course at her local church, she went on to administrate four courses on her campus during the following academic year.

Who is responsible for running your course?

We have three courses running this semester. I oversee Alpha as a whole and co-lead one of the courses.

What type of venue do you use for your Alpha for Students sessions?

Campus flats, chapel and chaplaincy room.

What format does your average session take?

Cakes, ice cream and drinks (no main meal – we just provide puddings)

Welcome and silly game

Video/talk

Loo break, tea, coffee and silly game

Discussion

What support or input have you had from other student organisations or churches?

A group from a local church came and did our weekend away for us – talks, worship, ministry etc. They were great. It was really nice to spend some time with 'older and wiser' Christians.

The CU has worked in conjunction with the Alpha team – financially, advertising, help with events and running. It has been a joint effort.

How did you first hear about Alpha for Students – and how did this encourage you to run a course yourself?

I came along to the Alpha for Students day in London and was really inspired to start a course at Roehampton. That is where it all took off.

Can you describe what happened from hearing about Alpha for Students until the point where you had your course ready to start?

I got involved with the CU and discussed my ideas with the leaders. We brought about nine people to the Alpha for Students Conference in September 2001. We spoke to the whole CU about our vision, opportunities for people to be involved, what Alpha is and how it works etc. We selected our team from people who were suitable and who had done the training. Those who had not done the training, but wanted to be involved, became our core team.

How did you prepare your team for the course?

We went to a London Alpha for Students training session. It really encouraged people, helped them to realise that you didn't need to be Nicky Gumbel to lead a group and that this was something that could provide a positive way of presenting the Christian message to our friends and course mates.

How did you launch your course – did you run an appetiser event?

Throughout Freshers' Week we handed out leaflets, postcards, drink mats, can of beans with Alpha labels replacing the beans labels all around campus, along with free lollipops. Posters went up everywhere, some with just the Alpha logo. We had a pizza night and someone gave the talk 'Christianity; Boring, Untrue and Irrelevant?' We had Alpha bags with *Why Jesus?* lollipops, *What is Alpha?* and information about when the course was running. Also, we set the CU the task of inviting and bringing their friends.

What happened on your weekend/day away?

Five guests went on the first weekend. Two became Christians. All loved it.

Did you run any type of celebration event at the end of your course to lead into the next one?

Yes, we went to a local karaoke noodle bar. One guest brought 10 friends! We didn't do a talk; I just explained what Alpha was and when the next course would be running.

Is there anything else you would like to tell us?

The feedback has been positive – people really are coming to Christ, Christians are recommending the course to friends, knowledge about the course is spreading, it's taking off!

Recently, about 50 of us went on the CU weekend away. Looking around, I counted eight people who were either on the current Alpha course or who had done Alpha in the autumn term, and I thought, 'Wow! It really works!' Members of the CU have seen the friends they bought along to Alpha become Christians and are realising that it is such a useful tool and an essential part of our vision to share our faith.

Tom Helyar-Cardwell is the Student Worker at the City Church Canterbury. Alpha for Students runs through the church but is held in people's homes.

What type of venue do you use for your Alpha for Students sessions?

Homes of people from the church.

What format does your average session take?

We started with an informal meal and chat, then a couple of worship songs, then watch the video and then split into three or so discussion groups.

Do you provide a meal or refreshments – if so, what type and how do you prepare it?

Yes – a proper meal each week but not eaten at a table. We have a team of three or four people who arrive at the house early to cook. We do simple student-friendly dishes.

What support have you had from other student organisations or churches?

Some of us went on the Alpha for Students Conference in September 2001. We also work closely with the CU on campus here (University of Kent) to promote the course.

How many times have you run Alpha for Students and when did you start?

Three times. The first course started in September 2000.

How did you first hear about Alpha for Students and how did this encourage you to run a course yourself?

Through the publicity for regular Alpha. We saw the course as a great way of assisting our evangelism to students.

Can you describe what happened from hearing about Alpha for Students until the point where you had your course ready to start?

We discussed the idea within the team, and asked some of the most committed students to help in the running of the course, although the student workers led it. We had a lot of support (financial, moral, prayer) from the church, and also from those who lent us their homes to use. We also worked closely with the Christian Union.

How did you prepare your team for the course?

We had an informal training session where we tried to pass on the main points covered in the Small Group Leaders seminar at the Alpha for Students Conference. However it was difficult getting everyone to attend and mostly we just gave advice ad hoc. Some more formal training would probably be a good idea in future.

How did you launch your course – did you run an appetiser event?

We spent four days on campus going through questionnaires with people about faith, belief etc, at the end of which we invited them to Alpha. This was done with the CU as part of their annual mission week. At the end of the week we held the Alpha introductory night in a lecture theatre, which was well promoted. Thereafter we moved the course into a house.

How many people came on your course on average?

About 35 guests came to the introductory night with about 17 committing to the course. They were a mixed group – mostly undergraduates. We also had a few international students from different ethnic groups and one mature student.

What happened on your weekend/day away?

We had a weekend away in Norfolk. We did the first Holy Spirit talk in the session proceeding the weekend to prepare people. On the Saturday we had the remaining two talks with ministry time after the second one in the evening. God really met with people and several made first time commitments. Others opened up much more to the reality of God and were prayed for. We also had a lot of time for relaxing social stuff. On the Sunday we had the 'How Do I Make the Most of the Rest of My Life?' talk.

Did you see any difference in your course when you returned from your weekend away?

Yes! More Christians, everyone more open, several began attending church. The group was also much closer and more united.

Did you run any type of celebration event at the end of your course to lead into the next one?

Yes, a reunion meal, where people could introduce their friends to the next Alpha course.

Which Alpha resources did you use for your course and how did you use them?

We used the videos for most of the talks except the first one and the weekend talks. We also had copies of *Searching Issues* and the accompanying individual booklets (eg *Suffering*) available for people to look at or borrow. We gave away a few Bibles to those that didn't have them.

Is there anything you would like to tell us?

Just that the course is proving a real success and seems to snowball. God seems to bless us more each time we run it. We find it is also good to run courses back to back to keep the momentum doing. The great thing with students is that they are so gregarious – people come on the course, tell others and often bring them too.

Now we have set the course in motion, more and more people are becoming interested and it has a high profile on campus.

Lindsey Redgate is a Student Worker with Christian Student Action (Agapé). She has administrated an Alpha for Students course that ran in the chaplaincy building at the University of Birmingham.

Who is responsible for running your course?

A couple of student workers together with five Christian students who are also committed to it. There are also two 'year-out' people from a local church involved.

What type of venue do you use for your Alpha for Students sessions?

Chaplaincy lounge.

What format does your average session take?

7pm	Start (people normally arrive at 7.15pm) – drinks and cake
7.45pm	Talk
8.00/8.05pm	Discussion groups
9pm	'Official' end of the evening, but then we invite them to stay and some of the students make more drinks for people

Do you provide a meal or refreshments?

Only drinks (tea, coffee, hot chocolate, squash) and home made cakes, brought by a different student every week. The guests love it! We always have a good laugh, especially when the boys have a turn – one even went home and got his mum to make it for him!

What support have you had from other student organisations or churches?

Support from Alpha for Students Office. From the Navigators in Birmingham – they had previously run Alpha courses in Birmingham so to begin with we worked with them, produced joint publicity and asked them lots of questions about the way they do it. From CU on campus – the individual hall groups supported it. From local churches – this second course was launched after an evangelistic event, which was supported by five local churches (two NFI, one Vineyard, one Elim, and one independent free church).

How did you first hear about Alpha for Students – and how did this encourage you to run a course yourself?

My team leader went to the Alpha for Students Conference in September 2001 and was inspired to try it here again! CSA had previously run Alpha a few years ago, which was not very successful – it was difficult to get people along.

Having more students involved as the core team and group leaders has been the main improvement this time – they have brought their friends, been faithful in praying for it and coming along, and made all the difference in credibility.

Can you describe what happened from hearing about Alpha for Students until the point where you had your course ready to start?

Following the Alpha for Students Conference, the CSA staff team talked about some of the experiences of other campuses and encouraged us to get behind trying it. We talked to the local Navigators group, who were already running Alpha, and found a suitable time for our course to make sure they were at different times to attract different people.

We ran a stall at Freshers' Week with the Navigators group. We spoke to the CU hall group leaders and they agreed to support it. Throughout Freshers' Week and the next two weeks they spoke to their CUs and identified a few key students who were particularly keen and willing to commit to the whole course. We had a training/get-to-know-you time and then launched the course with them as group leaders. We did the practical room booking, publicity etc, and organised the talks. We did most of the talk between us with the occasional outside speaker.

How did you prepare your team for the course?

We did some training before we started. It was difficult to get everyone together. We did one-to-one training with group leaders and with other individuals to help them understand Alpha and its philosophy. The first course was difficult because we had a few Christians who turned up with their friends and who hadn't had any Alpha training and wanted to preach in the open discussion bit.

How did you launch your course – did you run an appetiser event?

First course – we had a free meal.
Second course – we had the local churches' event, which was a live band in the Students' Union with a little talky bit and lots of Alpha publicity all round.

How many people came on your course?

First course – two guests became Christians on the course; two became Christians after the course during standard follow-up. The two others are also close now – I have been doing a Bible study with them and both have been reading their Bibles. They still have some questions but know much more now.

We are running our second course – eight non-Christians. We have found that most people are there by personal invitation and accompanied by a Christian friend. One girl has become a Christian recently. She came to the course with a friend; after three sessions her friend took her to church, where she gave her life to Christ. Some of the others are very close too.

Sarah Hart is a student. She co-leads an Alpha for Students course in her home for her fellow students at the University of Edinburgh

What type of venue do you use for your Alpha for Students sessions?

Flat.

What format does your average session take?

A cooked supper followed by a talk by a speaker; then a discussion, sometimes followed by a trip to a pub.

Where/how did you first hear about Alpha for Students – and how did this encourage you to run a course yourself?

The CU was running one but we had friends who found it too big and wanted something more personal.

Can you describe what happened from hearing about Alpha for Students until the point where you had your course ready to start?

A friend and I wanted to start up the course. We asked three friends who we thought may be interested, organised the course and prayer support, invited friends who we thought would be interested and those who asked us about it to come along.

How did you prepare your team for the course?

We used the Alpha training videos for the second course, which were really useful.

How did you launch your course – did you run an appetiser event?

We had two 'Christianity; Boring Untrue and Irrelevant?' talks at the flat with drinks beforehand for people we thought may be interested. Most of those who came to those did the course.

How did you advertise your course?

Word of mouth.

Please describe your first Alpha session.

We had a meal where we were able to get to know each other, then a speaker gave the talk, then he left us to discuss it without him there so everyone could feel more at ease. We found we split naturally into smaller groups where we discussed the issues raised and answered some of their questions.

What happened on your weekend/day away?

We went to stay in a cabin in the Scottish Borders with our speaker, his wife and their baby as well as the four leaders and four of the guests. We had a mix of talks, worship, informal chats, lots of food and long walks.

Did you see any difference in your course when you returned from your weekend away?

Everyone was far more relaxed with each other and able to ask questions more openly.

Is there anything you would like to tell us?

It was fantastic fun. We are all good friends now and all who came on the course are now really open to Christ or have returned to what had been a fledging faith.

Chapter 19

The challenge

They will know the truth, and the truth will set them free

Now that we have detailed all the facts and advice about running an Alpha for Students course, we hope that you are not overwhelmed. All your planning and care will undoubtedly provide an environment where students can relax, feel welcome and be open to hear the Christian message presented.

Alpha is essentially a tool to communicate the truth of the gospel to your guests. Be encouraged as you prepare; pray for your course; be committed to your student guests and trust that God will use your hard work to draw people into an exciting and life-changing relationship with him. *They will know the truth, and the truth will set them free.*

We hope that you will continue to use this manual and refer to the ideas and suggestions presented in it and that they will be helpful to you throughout all the stages of your course. Our vision is to have Alpha for Students on or near every university or college to offer every student the opportunity to attend a course and to hear the gospel presented to them in a non-threatening and relevant format.

It is such a privilege for us to hear how God is using this tool with students around the world. Time and time again we have seen God honour his promise to send his Spirit among us, and amazing and profound changes occur in lives as a result. We continue to see students give their lives to Christ, be filled with the Spirit and get excited about Jesus. We hope that you will find Alpha for Students an effective way to present the Christian message and we look forward to hearing how God works through your course.

Alpha for Students Office information

How we can help you

Alpha for Students Office
Alpha International
Holy Trinity Brompton
Brompton Road
London, SW7 1JA
United Kingdom

Telephone: **+44 (0)20 7581 8255**
Fax: **+44 (0)20 7584 8536**
E-mail: **alpha4students@htb.org.uk**
Website: **alphacourse.org**

The Alpha for Students Office is based at Holy Trinity Brompton in London and actively works with those running or interested in starting an Alpha for Students course. We work closely with students, churches and student workers to resource and support courses in whatever way we are able.

- **Advice** – if you have questions or challenges we would be keen to try and help you find a way around them.

- **Ideas** – being in contact with courses throughout the country means that we have accumulated knowledge about what works and what doesn't with Alpha for Students.

- **Resources** – producing materials to help courses.

- **Speakers** – we try to help courses to find speakers for their weekends away and weekly talks either by putting you in touch with Alpha Advisors and recommended speakers from local churches or by sending out speakers or teams from our church.

- **Training** – as with speakers, we try to help you cover your training needs wherever possible.

- **Conferences** – every year we hold an Alpha for Students conference in London. We highly recommend that all courses consider bringing their entire team to be equipped and envisioned and to capture or refresh the vision for using Alpha to reach students.

- **Alpha for Students Days** – we are arranging regional days throughout the UK, to provide help and encouragement to both those running courses and those who have no experience of Alpha. Watch out for a day near you!

- **Prayer** – let us know when you will be running your course, weekend away or appetiser and we will pray for you.

- **Support** – as you run your course we would love to support you in whatever other ways you need.

Please keep in touch – we would be thrilled to hear about your successes and your challenges and support you as you reach out to students in your area.

Mission Statement

To introduce Alpha into every university and place of further education so that every student has the opportunity to attend an Alpha course

Appendix B

Suggested Resources

What you need to run a course

Based on a course with 30 guests and 10 helpers

Essential items	ISBN Number*	Normal Price*	Price with Student Discount**
Alpha for Students Introductory Video	1-9040-7420-0	£4.99	£1.65
The A–Z of Running Alpha for Students (manual)	1-9040-7429-4	£5.99	£1.98
Alpha Team Training Manual (x10)	1-8988-3801-1	£15.00	£4.95
Alpha Team Training Video	1-8988-3815-1	£14.99	£4.95
Alpha Manual (x30)	1-8988-3800-3	£45.00	£14.85
Why Jesus? (x30)	1-8988-3845-3	£12.00	£3.96
Drinks Mats (x200)	1-9029-7075-6	£10.00	£3.30
Invitations (x250)	HTB-B19	£25.00	£8.25
A4 Posters (x50)	HTB-B15	£25.00	£8.25
~ Searching Issues (x5)	HTB05	£24.95	£8.23
~ Questions of Life (x5)	HTB04	£29.95	£9.88
Total Cost		**£211.87**	**£69.92**

Optional items	ISBN Number*	Normal Price*	Price with Student Discount**
Alpha course on video	1-8988-3862-3	£89.95	£29.68
Alpha for Students Introductory Guide	1-9027-5086-1	£1.50	£0.50
Developing Ministry on Alpha (video)	1-9027-5003-9	£8.99	£2.97
Prayer and Alpha (video)	1-9027-5002-0	£8.99	£2.97
Worship on Alpha Pack	1-8988-3841-0	£20.00	£6.60
~ Why Does God Allow Suffering?	HTB103	£0.99	£0.33
~ What About Other Religions?	HTB104	£0.99	£0.33
~ 30 Days (Introduction to reading the Bible)	1-8988-3880-1	£2.50	£0.82
Alpha Cookbook	1-8988-3807-0	£5.99	£1.98

* Please note that these references and prices were accurate at time of printing.
** The 67 per cent student discount applies to courses run by students in the UK. International courses should register with the UK Alpha for Students Office to be eligible for the discount when ordering English resources through the UK distributor.
~ These resources could be sold during the course.

To order within the UK, telephone 0845 7581 278 quoting your course reference number (to obtain your 67 per cent discount if eligible). If you are outside the UK, please contact the Alpha for Students Office for specific advice on how to order resources in your country.

Appendix C

Fitting Alpha into your term or semester

Possible course programmes

Standard course

This would be the first and ideal choice for your course programme; however, it is likely that you will have insufficient time within your term or semester to fit it in. If this is the case, see the following 8, 9 and 10 week course programme suggestions to help you find the appropriate programme for you.

Optional:

Introductory session   Appetiser Event: *Christianity: Boring, Untrue and Irrelevant?*

Week 1   *Who Is Jesus?*
Week 2   *Why Did Jesus Die?*

Week 3   *How Can I Be Sure of My Faith?*
Week 4   *Why and How Should I Read the Bible?*
Week 5   *Why and How Do I Pray?*
Week 6   *How Does God Guide Us?*

Weekend away:
Who Is the Holy Spirit?
What Does the Holy Spirit Do?
How Can I Be Filled With the Holy Spirit?
How Can I Make the Most of the Rest of My Life?

Week 7   *How Can I Resist Evil?*
Week 8   *Why and How Should We Tell Others?*
Week 9   *Does God Heal Today?*
Week 10   *What About the Church?*

Optional:

Week 11   Celebration Event: *Christianity: Boring, Untrue and Irrelevant?*

Eight weeks
New course or first course after a long break

Week 1   Appetiser Event: *Christianity: Boring, Untrue and Irrelevant?*
Week 2   *Who Is Jesus?*
Week 3   *Why Did Jesus Die?*
Week 4   *How Can I Be Sure of My Faith?*
Week 5   *How Do God and I Communicate*? (Combination of *'Why and How
                  Should I Read the Bible?'* and *'Why and How Do I Pray?'*)

                  Weekend away: including extra talk *How Does God Guide Us?*
                  (See standard course for weekend talks.)

Week 6   *How Can I Resist Evil?*
Week 7   **Why and How Should We Tell Others?* and *Does God Heal Today?*
                  (Combined talk)
Week 8   ** What About the Church?*

* Alternatively you could combine *'Why and How Should We Tell Others?'* and *'What About the Church?'* in Week 8 after *'Does God Heal Today?'* in Week 7.

Follow-up course as part of rolling programme

Week 1   *Who Is Jesus?*
Week 2   *Why Did Jesus Die?*
Week 3   *How Can I Be Sure of My Faith?*
Week 4   *How Do God and I Communicate?* (Combination of *'Why and How
                  Should I Read the Bible?'* and *'Why and How Do I Pray?'*)
Week 5   *How Does God Guide Us?*

                  Weekend away (See standard course for weekend talks.)

Week 6	*How Can I Resist Evil?*
Week 7	*Combination of two of the following talks: 'Why and How Should We Tell Others?' 'Does God Heal Today?' 'What About the Church?'*
Week 8	Celebration Event: *Christianity: Boring, Untrue and Irrelevant?*

* The talk that you omit could easily be covered on a separate occasion in a more informal setting or as the beginning to a follow-up group during the following term.

Nine weeks
New course or first course after a long break

Week 1	Appetiser Event: *Christianity: Boring, Untrue and Irrelevant?*
Week 2	*Who Is Jesus?*
Week 3	*Why Did Jesus Die?*
Week 4	*How Can I Be Sure of My Faith?*
Week 5	*How Do God and I Communicate?* (Combination of *'Why and How Should I Read the Bible?'* and *'Why and How Do I Pray?'*)
Week 6	*How Does God Guide Us?*
	Weekend away (See standard course for weekend talks.)
Week 7	*How Can I Resist Evil?*
Week 8	*Why and How Should We Tell Others?* and *Does God Heal Today?* (Combined talk)
Week 9	*What About the Church?*

* Alternatively you can combine *'Why and How Should We Tell Others?'* and *'What About the Church?'* in Week 9 after *'Does God Heal Today?'* in Week 8.

Follow-up course as part of rolling programme

Week 1	*Who Is Jesus?*
Week 2	*Why Did Jesus Die?*
Week 3	*How Can I Be Sure of My Faith?*
Week 4	*How Do God and I Communicate?* (Combination of *'Why and How Should I Read the Bible?'* and *'Why and How Do I Pray?'*)
Week 5	*How Does God Guide Us?*
	Weekend away (See standard course for weekend talks.)
Week 6	*How Can I Resist Evil?*
Week 7	*Why and How Should We Tell Others?* and *Does God Heal Today?* (Combined talk)
Week 8	*What About the Church?*
Week 9	Celebration Event: *Christianity: Boring, Untrue and Irrelevant?*

* Alternatively you can combine *'Why and How Should We Tell Others?'* and *'What About the Church?'* in Week 8 after *'Does God Heal Today?'* in Week 7.

Ten weeks
New course or first course after a long break

Week 1	Appetiser Event (with *Christianity: Boring, Untrue and Irrelevant?*)
Week 2	*Who Is Jesus?*
Week 3	*Why Did Jesus Die?*
Week 4	*How Can I Be Sure of My Faith?*
Week 5	*How Do God and I Communicate?* (Combination of *'Why and How Should I Read the Bible?'* and *'Why and How Do I Pray?'*)
Week 6	*How Does God Guide Us?*
	Weekend away (See standard course for weekend talks.)

Week 7	*How Can I Resist Evil?*
Week 8	*Why and How Should We Tell Others?*
Week 9	*Does God Heal Today?*
Week 10	*What About the Church?*

Follow-up course as part of rolling programme

Week 1	*Who is Jesus?*
Week 2	*Why Did Jesus Die?*
Week 3	*How Can I Be Sure of My Faith?*
Week 4	*How Do God and I Communicate?* (Combination of *'Why and How Should I Read the Bible?'* and *'Why and How Do I Pray?'*)
Week 5	*How Does God Guide Us?*
	Weekend away (See standard course for weekend talks.)
Week 6	*How Can I Resist Evil?*
Week 7	*Why and How Should We Tell Others?*
Week 8	*Does God Heal Today?*
Week 9	*What About the Church?*
Week 10	Celebration Event: *Christianity: Boring, Untrue and Irrelevant?*

Over two terms

It is important to emphasise that we do not recommend running courses with a break in the middle unless absolutely necessary.

If you have to split your course to work around very short terms or to use Alpha as a follow-up to a mission type of event we would encourage you to consider the following points and suggestions. If you have any further questions please contact the Alpha for Students Office for advice on your specific situation.

- **Weekend/Day away**

Wherever possible run your weekend BEFORE you have a break in your course. Your guests are more likely to come away with you before you all disappear for a break than after you return.

- **After the break**

In the Alpha training we emphasise the importance of not chasing your guests to return the following week. However, it would be worthwhile your leaders establishing good methods of communication throughout the break without giving the appearance of pursuing someone simply to return to the course. A great deal of sensitivity is required in this area and each individual relationship should be considered independently.

Suggested timetable

Week 1	*Appetiser Event: *Christianity: Boring, Untrue and Irrelevant?*
Week 2	*Who Is Jesus?*
Week 3	*Why Did Jesus Die?*
Week 4	*How Can I Be Sure of My Faith?*
Week 5	*How Do God and I Communicate?* (Combination of *'Why and How Should I Read the Bible?'* and *'Why and How Do I Pray?'*)
	Weekend away (See standard course for weekend talks)
Week 6	*How Does God Guide Us?*
	Break
Week 7	*How Can I Resist Evil?*
Week 8	*Why and How Should We Tell Others?*
Week 9	*Does God Heal Today?*
Week 10	*What About the Church?*
Week 11	*Celebration Event: *Christianity: Boring, Untrue and Irrelevant?*

* If you are forced to spilt your course over two terms you could run either an appetiser or celebration event (or both) depending on the total number of weeks you have available and when your next course will begin.

Weekend Away programmes

Suggestions to help plan your weekend or day away

Full weekend programme (Friday to Saturday)

Friday

20.00   Guests arrive and settle in

20.30   Meal (something that can be kept warm for late arrivals) – with welcome and joke

21.30   Social (eg pub, games)

Saturday

9.30   Breakfast

10.30   Welcome, joke and worship

10.45   TALK: *Who Is the Holy Spirit?*

11.30   Coffee

12.00   TALK: *What Does the Holy Spirit Do?*

12.45   Session ends

13.00   Lunch

13.45   Discussion groups

14.30   Free time

18.00   Evening meal

19.00   Joke and worship

19.15   TALK: *How Can I Be Filled With the Holy Spirit?*

21.00   Social time

Sunday

9.00   Breakfast

9.45   Discussion groups

10.30   Coffee

11.00   Joke and worship

11.15   TALK: *How Can I Make the Most of the Rest of My Life?* (If appropriate, Holy Communion may be taken following this talk and ministry)

13.00   Lunch

14.00   Pack up and depart

Two day programme (Saturday to Sunday)

Saturday

10.30   ARRIVE – Coffee and settle in

10.45   Welcome, joke and worship

11.00   TALK: *Who Is the Holy Spirit?*

11.45   Coffee

12.00   TALK: *What Does the Holy Spirit Do?*

12.45   Session ends

13.00   Lunch

13.45   Discussion groups

14.30   Free time

18.00   Evening meal

19.00   Joke and worship

19.15   TALK: *How Can I Be Filled With the Holy Spirit?*

21.00   Social time

Sunday

9.00   Breakfast

9.45   Discussion groups

10.30   Coffee

11.00   Joke and worship

11.15   TALK: *How Can I Make the Most of the Rest of My Life?* (If appropriate, Holy Communion may be taken following this talk and ministry)

13.00   Lunch

14.00   Pack up and depart

One day programme

9.30	Coffee
10.00	Welcome, joke and worship
10.15	TALKS (combined): *Who Is the Holy Spirit?* and *What Does the Holy Spirit Do?*
11.00	Coffee and discussion groups (optional)
11.30	Joke and worship
11.45	TALK: *How Can I Be Filled With the Holy Spirit?*
13.30	Lunch
14.00	Free time
16.00	Discussion groups – with hot drinks (optional)
16.45	Joke and worship
17.00	TALK: *How Can I Make the Most of the Rest of My Life?* (If appropriate, Holy Communion may be taken following this talk and ministry)
19.00	Day ends

Alternative afternoon (depending upon venue and time available)

17.00	Discussion groups – with hot drinks (optional)
18.00	Evening meal
19.00	Joke and worship
19.15	TALK: *How Can I Make the Most of the Rest of My Life?*
21.00	Day ends

Appendix E

Alternative programmes

Ideas of how you might fit your Alpha sessions into a difficult timeslot

By now you should have an idea of the time of day you plan to run your Alpha for Students sessions. Below are programme ideas, which might help you to keep to the Alpha recipe, while making some subtle changes to the timing. These are intended as a guide to help you estimate the timings for your Alpha sessions and ensure that you allow the right amount of time for the three key parts of the course.

Standard evening
For the standard Alpha evening programme please see Chapter 7.

Shortened evening (where no meal is possible)

19.00	*Team prayer meeting*	*To pray, encourage the team, discuss the content of the video/talk, answer any questions and cover administrative issues. You could shorten the meeting after the first few weeks of the course to half an hour.*
19.45	**Session starts, coffee served**	Guests arrive, leaders and helpers are ready to welcome their guests as they arrive and to serve them coffee. Guests remain in small groups.
20.00	**Welcome, joke**	Course leader welcomes everyone and tells a joke to help guests relax.
20.10	**Worship**	To introduce guests to the practice of corporate worship.
20.15	**Talk**	To present the guests with information through a factual and well-presented talk (you will need live speakers to shorten the talks – see Chapter 12).
20.45	**Small group discussion**	To allow guests to discuss in an unthreatening, non-confrontational and accepting environment.
21.30	**End**	Group leaders should be prepared to summarise the discussion and close the session promptly.
Après-Alpha	*Time permitting*	*You may continue chatting in a more relaxed environment with those who want to go on to somewhere else (whatever would be the most natural activity for your guests).*

Lunchtime

11.30	*Team prayer meeting*	*To pray, encourage the team, discuss the content of the video/talk, answer any questions and cover administrative issues. You could shorten the meeting after the first few weeks or hold it earlier in the day.*
12.00	**Session starts, meal served, eaten**	Guests arrive, leaders and helpers are ready to welcome their guests as they arrive. Food is eaten in small groups while relationships are built.
12.20	**Welcome, joke, worship**	Course leader welcomes guests and tells a joke to put them at ease. Worship is optional depending on time available
12.30	**Talk**	To present the guests with information through a factual and well-presented talk (live speakers will be needed to deliver a shortened talk – see Chapter 12).
13.00	**Coffee, small group discussion**	To help guests relax over a hot drink and move easily into the group discussion.
13.45	**End**	Group leaders should be prepared to summarise the discussion and close the session promptly to allow guests to get away to their next lecture etc.
Après-Alpha	*Time permitting*	*You may continue chatting in a more relaxed environment with those who want to go on to somewhere else (whatever would be the most natural activity for your guests).*

Breakfast

7.00	*Team prayer meeting*	*To pray, encourage the team, discuss the content of the video/talk, answer any questions and cover administrative issues. You can shorten the meeting after the first few weeks.*
7.30	**Session starts, coffee and breakfast served**	Guests arrive, leaders and helpers are ready to welcome their guests as they arrive and to help them get their breakfast. Food is eaten in small groups while relationships are built.
7.45	**Welcome, joke**	Course leader welcomes guests and tells a joke to put them at ease.
7.50	**Talk**	To present the guests with information through a factual and well-presented talk *(live speakers will be needed to deliver a shortened talk – see Chapter 12).*
8.20	**Coffee or tea, Small group discussion**	To help guests relax over a hot drink and move easily into the group discussion.
8.50	**End**	Group leaders should be prepared to summarise the discussion and close the session promptly to allow guests to get away to their lectures etc.
Après-Alpha	*Time permitting*	*You may continue chatting in a more relaxed environment with those who want to go on to somewhere else (whatever would be the most natural activity for your guests).*

Appendix F

Suggested song list

Ideas for worship

The below song list will give you an idea of what might work as you plan the songs to introduce and repeat throughout the course, as well as increasing the length of your worship. It is not essential that you follow these songs exactly.

Week 1   *Praise To The Lord The Almighty (hymn)*
           Give Thanks With A Grateful Heart

Week 2   *Give Thanks With A Grateful Heart*
           When I Survey The Wondrous Cross (hymn)

Week 3   *Here Is Love Vast As The Ocean (hymn)*
           Amazing Grace (hymn)

Week 4   *I Lift My Eyes Up*
           Here Is Love

Week 5   *Praise God From Whom All Blessings Flow*
           Every Day I Look To You
           I Lift My Eyes Up

Week 6   *Praise God From Whom All Blessings Flow*
           Give Your Thanks To The Risen Son
           Every Day I Look To You
           Lead Me Lord

Weekend onwards

By this stage of the course, most guests will be opening up to the idea and practice of worship. We suggest that you now start to move the worship on with songs that would be most suitable to the guests on your course depending on the stage that they have reached.

The *Alpha Worship Pack* is available with more detailed guidelines and help for your worship leader. This would be especially useful if they have never seen the Alpha course modelled or are relatively inexperienced at leading worship.

See Appendix B for details on how to order your 'Alpha Worship Pack' and other resources.

Feedback questionnaire
(end of course)

Finding out what people think

Alpha for Students **Questionnaire**

Name   Group
_____   _____

1. How did you hear about the Alpha course?
_____
_____
_____

2. Why did you decide to do Alpha?
_____
_____
_____

3. How many sessions did you attend?
_____

4.a Were you a Christian when you started the course?
_____

Were you a regular churchgoer when you started the course?
_____
_____

b How would you describe yourself now (in terms of the Christian faith)?
_____

c If the answer to a and b is different, when and how did the change occur?
_____
_____
_____

5. In what ways, if any, did you benefit from doing the Alpha course?

_____

_____

_____

6. What did you enjoy most about Alpha?

_____

_____

7. What did you find most difficult?

_____

_____

_____

8. Which, if any, tapes did you buy?

_____

9. Which, if any, books did you buy?

_____

10. Did you find them helpful and if so why?

    (please name any books or tapes that you found particularly helpful)

_____

11.   In what way could the course be improved?

    a   Talks

_____

_____

    b   Small groups

_____

_____

    c   Generally

_____

_____

12.   Any other comments

_____

_____

Are you planning to get involved with any other Christian group/church at the end of the course? If so, where?

Appendix H

Course registration form

Letting us know you are out there

AlphaforStudents

Alpha

Use this form to register your Alpha for Students course if it is not already listed in the Alpha for Students Course Directory in *Alpha News*.

Registering your course is free and enables us to list it in *Alpha News* and on our website. Information from the shaded boxes on this form will be placed on our website and given to anyone looking for a local Alpha for Students course.

Course contact

Title:

First name:

Surname:

Are you a:
☐ Student
☐ Student worker
☐ Chaplain
☐ Other

Year of graduation:

Organisation/church:

University:

Termtime address:

Town/city:

County/province:

Postal code:

Country:

Telephone:

Mobile:

E-mail:

Home address (if different to above):

Town/city:

County/province:

Postal code:

Country:

Telephone:

Mobile:

E-mail:

Church details (if applicable)

Name of church:

Denomination:

Church leader:

Mailing address:

County/province:

Postal code:

Country:

Telephone:

E-mail:

Course details

Course name (eg. University of Essex CU Alpha for Students):

University(ies):

Course town (as you would prefer it listed in *Alpha News*):

Course county/province:

Course postal code:

Course country:

Course E-mail:

Course website:

Date of first Alpha course:

How many times has this organisation run Alpha?

How do you give the Alpha course talks?   Videos

Own speakers   Audio tapes   Combination

Which of the following best describes your course venue?

Home   Campus   Halls of residence   Local church   Other

Data Protection Policy
The information you provide on this form will only be used for purposes
directly connected with the Alpha course. We never sell, rent or loan your
personal information to others, although we sometimes pass your details to our
Alpha Advisers and local conference organisers. We hold your details on
computer under the terms of the Data Protection Act 1998.

❑ If you would prefer your details not to be given to our trusted Alpha
Advisers and local conference organisers for Alpha related activities only,
please tick this box.

❑ Please tick here if you don't want your name and daytime telephone number
to be listed on our website search facility.

Appendix I

National Offices

Alpha contact worldwide

Alpha International Head Office

Alpha International

Holy Trinity Brompton
Brompton Road
London, SW7 1JA
United Kingdom

Tel: +44 (0)20 7581 8255
Fax: +44 (0)20 7584 8536
E-mail: Info@alphacourse.org
Website: alphacourse.org

Alpha Australia

PO Box 57
Hunters Hill
NSW 2110
Australia

Tel: +61 (0)2 9816 5477
Fax: +61 (0)2 9816 5795
E-mail: admin@alphaaustralia.org.au
Website: alphaaustralia.org.au

Alpha Austria

Alpha Osterreich
Riedenburger Strasse 8
5020 Salzburg
Austria

Tel: +43 (0)662 84 08 04
Fax: +43 (0)662 84 08 04
E-mail: alphabuero@utanet.at
Website: alphakurs.at

Alpha Canada

Alpha Ministries Canada
Box 153
3456 Dunbar Street
Vancouver
BC V6S 2C2
Canada

Tel: +1 800 743 0899 or 604 224 0067
Fax: +1 604 224 6124
E-mail: office@alphacanada.org
Website: alphacanada.org

Alpha Denmark

Alpha Danmark
Karlslunde Mosevej 3
2690 Karlslunde
Denmark

Tel: +45 4615 0188
Fax: +45 4615 0117
E-mail: alpha.danmark@mail.dk
Website: alphadanmark.dk

Alpha Finland

PL 198
13101 Hameenlinna
Finland

Tel: +358 (0)40 563 2225
Fax: +358 (0)19 246 1422
E-mail: alfa@svk.fi

Alpha France

BP 18
78780 Maurecourt
France

Tel: +33 (0)1 39 70 51 14
Fax: +33 (0)1 39 70 41 03
E-mail: contact@alpha-france.org

Alpha Germany

Alpha Deutschland
Nieder Kirchweg 7
65934 Frankfurt
Germany

Tel: +49 (0)69 38778591
Fax: +49 69 38778593
E-mail: office@alphakurs.de
Website: alpha.tcf.de

Alpha Hong Kong

Alpha Course Hong Kong Ltd
3305 Tower One
Lippo Centre
89 Queensway
Hong Kong

Tel: +852 2869 1066
Fax: +852 2869 1313
E-mail: hkalpha@alpha.org.hk
Website: alpha.org.hk

Alpha Hungary
Kisteteny u 33
Budapest
1223
Hungary

Tel: +36 (0)1 362 60 17
Fax: +36 (0)1 362 62 80
E-mail: tamtun@freemail.hu

Alpha Japan
Matsuo Building 7F
1-25-3 Hongo Bunkyo Ku
Tokyo 113-0033
Japan

Tel: +81 (0)3 3868 8775
Fax: +81 (0)3 3868 8776
E-mail: info@alphajapan.jp

Alpha New Zealand
PO Box 26 119
Wellington
New Zealand

Tel: +64 (0)4 477 3997
Fax: +64 (0)4 477 3927
E-mail: info@alpha.org.nz
Website: alpha.org.nz

Alpha India
Plot No 512
Road 30
Jubilee Hills
Hyderabad
500 033
India

Tel: +91 40 355 3127
Fax: +91 40 355 3138
E-mail: ymcadavid@yahoo.com

Alpha Kenya
13 Mamlaka Court
Mamlaka Road – nr Serena Hotel
opp Nairobi Chapel
PO Box 63524 Muthaiga
Nairobi
Kenya

Tel: +254 (0)2 243731 or 513305
Fax: +254 (0)2 513305
E-mail: gathoni@hillandfoster.com

Alpha Norway
Alpha Norge
Bergelandsgt 30
4012 Stavanger
Norway

Tel: +47 51 53 15 80
Fax: +47 51 89 56 16
E-mail: alphanor@online.no

Alpha Ireland
Bellmount House Ballinea
Mullingar
Co Westmeath
Ireland

Tel: +353 (0)44 45454
Fax: +353 (0)44 49670
E-mail: vmcgillycuddy@eircom.net
Website: alphacourse.ie

Alpha Netherlands
IZB Bookshop
Johan van Oldenbarneveltlaan 10
3818 HB Amersfoort
Netherlands

Tel: +31 (0)33 461 1949
Fax: +31 (0)33 465 9204
E-mail: info@alpha-cursus.nl
Website: alpha-cursus.nl

Alpha Romania
CP15 14-24
Constanta
8700
Romania

Tel: +40 (0)41 55 23 59
E-mail: alfa.ro@impromex.ro

Alpha Russia

16 Parkovaya 37-1-198
105484 Moscow
Russia

Tel: +7 095 963 3511
Fax: +7 095 963 3511
E-mail: alpha@i4j.net
Website: i4j.net/alpha/

Alpha South Korea

Seorosarang Love One Another
Book Publishing,   Seolim Building
919-7 Bangbae-1Dong
Seocho-Ku,   Seoul 137-061
South Korea

Tel: +82 (0)2 586 9211
Fax: +82 (0)2 586 9215
E-mail: sarang@alphakorea.org
Website: alphakorea.org

Alpha USA

9th Floor
74 Trinity Place
New York
NY
USA

Tel: +1 212 406 5269
Fax: +1 212 406 7521
E-mail: info@alphausa.org
Website: alphana.org

Alpha Singapore

St Johns – St Margarets Church
30 Dover Avenue
Singapore

Tel: +65 6774 5743
Fax: +65 6779 5673
E-mail: info@alpha.org.sg
Website: alpha.org.sg

Alpha Sweden

Alpha Sverige
Kummelby Kyrka
Box 13
19121 Sollentuna
Sweden

Tel: +46 8 35 18 62
Fax: +46 46 8 50 55 14 34
E-mail: info@alphasverige.org
Website: alphasverige.org

Alpha Zambia

Anglican Cathedral of the Holy
Cross
PO Box 30477
Lusaka
Zambia

Tel: +260 1 250484 or 220827
Fax: +260 1 250 228
E-mail: alfredt@zamnet.zm

Alpha South Africa

PO Box 784
Parklands
Johannesburg 2121
South Africa

Tel: +27 (0)11 341 0551
Fax: +27 (0)11 341 0551
E-mail: inform@alphasa.co.za
Website: www.alphasa.co.za

Alpha Switzerland

Alphalive Schweiz
Josefstrasse 206
8005 Zurich
Switzerland

Tel: +41 (0)1 274 8474
Fax: +41 (0)1 274 8483
E-mail: info@alphalive.ch
Website: alphalive.ch

Alpha Zimbabwe

Alpha Ministries Zimbabwe
PO Box A1918
Avondale
Harare
Zimbabwe

Tel: +263 (0)4 339697
Fax: +263 (0)4 339697
E-mail: avnalpha@mango.zw

Appendix J

Jokes

Put your guests at ease

These are a few suggestions to help you if you are struggling to find your own jokes. Please feel free to use better ones – unfortunately we can't guarantee that you will get a laugh (nor can we guarantee that they are funny!)

Here goes…

The Texan and the swimming pool

(great for your first week)

I heard about a wealthy Texan who had a huge estate in Texas. Actually, they wouldn't call it an estate there; they would call it a ranch. He had a huge ranch in Texas where he had a big floodlit swimming pool and in this swimming pool he kept a shark. That's a very important part of the story. So in this huge floodlit swimming pool he kept a shark. And what he loved to do was throw lavish dinner parties and to invite his guests up around the pool afterwards. Then he would say to them, 'If any of you will swim a length of this pool I will give you one of three things: $10 million, half of my estate, or the hand of my daughter in marriage.'

He always said before he finished, 'but I must warn you before you do so, there is a shark in the pool.'

Well one evening as he was saying this, there was a splash, and a man, very smartly dressed, swam the entire length of the pool chased by the shark. He got out of the pool just in time as the shark thudded into the wall.

The Texan said, 'Congratulations you are the first person who has ever done that. Now what would you like? Would you like $10 million?'

The man said, 'No thank you.'

He said, 'Would you like half of my estate?'

The man said, 'No thank you.'

He said, 'Ahh, you want the hand of my daughter in marriage?'

The man said, 'No thank you.'

So the Texan said to him, 'Well what do you want?'

He said, 'I want the name of the person who pushed me in.'

The bishop speaking at the Mothers' Union

I heard about a Bishop who had the habit that whenever he told a joke he would forget the punch-line. Because of this, he never ever told jokes because he felt too afraid that he would forget the funny part.

On one occasion he was invited by the Mothers' Union to talk at the Albert Hall. Now if you speak to the Mothers' Union you really do have to start with a joke.

So he went to his chaplain and said, 'Help, what do I do? I just don't know any jokes at all. Can you help me?'

So the Chaplain said to him, 'Yes, I've got exactly the one for you. When you get up start your talk like this, say, "The happiest years of my life were spent in the arms of another man's wife," pause dramatically and then say, 'that was my father's wife' (in other words his mother) and then they will all laugh very loudly.' (To audience) just like you did then!

So the great moment came and he got up to speak and

he started his talk, 'The happiest years of my life were spent in the arms of another man's wife' and he paused. Then he said, 'I can't remember for the life of me whose wife she was!'

Revelation 3, verse 20 and Genesis 3, verse 10

I heard about a rural vicar who was visiting one of his parishioners – a middle-aged woman and she was living in a cottage somewhere. He went to the door, he rang the doorbell and there was no response. He could see there was a light on so he rang again, but again there was no response. He went round to see and there was a radio on and a light was on and so he thought, 'This is funny… well, I'll just leave a note.' Revelation 3, verse 20 came to mind and he wrote a little note to her saying; 'Behold I stand at the door and knock, if anyone hears my voice and opens the door, I will come in and eat with them and they with me.' He thought this was a very appropriate verse and he put it through the letterbox and off he went.

The following Sunday he saw the woman in church. She came up to him and just handed him a little note and when he looked at his note he saw that she had also written a verse on her note. She had written this: Genesis 3, verse 10, 'I heard you in the garden, and I was afraid, because I was naked, so I hid.'

Johnny's prayer *(Why and How Do I Pray?)*

Tonight's subject is prayer and some people are very proud of the fact that they don't pray. Others are proud of the fact that they do pray.
I heard of one family which was very proud of the fact

that they did pray and very proud of the fact that they brought their children up to pray. One time they had some visitors coming to lunch and they wanted to sort of boast, show-off to their visitors how well they had brought up their children and how their children prayed.

So when it came to lunch they said to the little boy Johnny, 'Johnny, why don't you pray?' Johnny looked rather embarrassed and he said, 'I can't.' So, the mother just whispered to him, 'Darling, just say what daddy said at breakfast.' So he shut his eyes and said, 'Oh God [pause] we've got these dreadful people coming to lunch.'

Church notices *(How Does God Guide Us?)*

One of the things about the church is that sometimes we sent out confusing messages… it is often our fault that we don't put the message across very clearly. This is particularly true in church notices. I don't know whether you are familiar with the sort of notices that are given in churches, but someone made a list of some of the notices that have gone out. These are actual printed church notices, let me give you some examples.

One church had this, 'This afternoon there will be a meeting in the south and north ends of the church. Children will be baptised at both ends.'

Another one wrote this, 'Tuesday at 4pm there will be an ice-cream social. All ladies giving milk come early.'

'Thursday at 5pm there will be a meeting of the Little Mothers' Club. All ladies wishing to be Little Mothers please meet the pastor in the study.'

'This being Easter Sunday, we will ask Mr Johnson to come forward and lay an egg at the altar.'

'The service will close with Little Drop of Water. One of the ladies will start quietly and then the rest of the congregation will join in.'

'On Sunday a special collection will be taken to defray the expenses of the new carpet. All those wishing to do something on the new carpet, come forward and get a piece of paper.'

Another church had this; 'The ladies of the church have cast off clothing of every kind and may be seen in the church basement Friday afternoon.'

Another church had this notice, 'A bean supper will be held on Saturday evening in the church basement. Music will follow.'

Finally this, 'Tonight's sermon: "What is hell?" Come early and listen to our choir practice.'

The lawyers' questions

The question is, 'Is Christianity, Boring, Untrue and Irrelevant?' It is so important to ask the right questions. I think the people who are the most notorious at asking stupid questions are probably lawyers. I came across some of the cross-examinations that have taken place. These are actual cross-examinations that have taken place in American courts and they are reported by the Massachusetts Bar Association lawyers' journal. These are some questions asked by lawyers and some insightful answers given by some of the witnesses.

Question: 'She had three children, right?'
Answer: 'Yes.'
Question: 'How many were boys?'
Answer: 'None.'
Question: 'Were there any girls?'

Question: 'Can you describe the individual?'
Answer: 'He was about medium height and had a beard.'
Question: 'Was this a male or a female?'

Question: 'Doctor, how many autopsies have you performed on dead people?'
Answer: 'All my autopsies are performed on dead people.'

Question: 'All your responses must be oral, okay? What school did you go to?'
Answer: 'Oral.'

Question: 'Do you recall the time when you examined the body?'
Answer: 'The autopsy started around 8.30pm.'
Question: 'And Mr Dennington was dead at the time?'
Answer: 'No he was sitting on the table wondering why I was doing an autopsy.'

Question: 'Doctor, before you performed the autopsy did you check for a pulse?'
Answer: 'No.'
Question: 'Did you check for blood pressure?'
Answer: 'No.'
Question: 'Did you check for breathing?'
Answer: 'No.'
Question: 'So then it is possible that the patient was alive when you began the autopsy?'

Answer: 'No'

Question: 'How can you be so sure, doctor?'

Answer: 'Because his brain was sitting on my desk in a jar.'

Question: 'Ah, but could the patient have been alive nevertheless?'

Answer: 'It is possible, he could have been alive and practising law somewhere.'

The police exam

(How Can I Make the Most of the Rest of My Life?)

It's very hard to be different. I heard of a young police officer who was taking his final exam at Hendon Police College in North London. In the exam paper there were four questions. The first three were relatively easy and he answered them without any problem. Then this young police officer got to question four and this is how question four read:

'You are on patrol in outer London when an explosion occurs in a gas main in a nearby street. On investigation you discover that a large hole has been blown in the footpath and there is an overturned van lying nearby. Inside the van there is a strong smell of alcohol, both occupants, a man and a woman, are injured. You recognise the woman as the wife of your divisional inspector who is at present away in the United States of America. A passing motorist stops to give you assistance and you realise that he is a man that is wanted for armed robbery. Suddenly a man runs out of a nearby house, shouting that a woman is expecting a baby and that the shock of the explosion has made the birth imminent. Another man is shouting for help having been blown into an adjacent canal by the explosion and he cannot swim.'

The question goes on, 'Bearing in mind the provisions of the Mental Health Act describe in a few words what actions you would take.'

Well the officer thought about this for a few moments, he picked up his pen and then he wrote this: 'I would take off my uniform and mingle with the crowd.'

Appendix K

Alpha copyright
Using Alpha

The Directors of Alpha International write: 'We have always been keen to allow individuals who are running an Alpha course the flexibility to adapt where it was felt necessary to allow for locally felt needs and where there was the desire to retain the essential elements, nature and identity of the course. Experience has shown though that this has been misunderstood and the resulting loss of integrity in some courses has given rise to considerable confusion. Now that Alpha is running all around the world we have reluctantly had to draw up a copyright statement more tightly to preserve confidence and quality control. We are sure you will understand.'

1. With the exception of books published by Kingsway (in which the author is stated to hold the copyright), all Alpha resources and materials including booklets, tapes and graphics are copyright to Alpha International.

2. In no circumstances may any part of any Alpha resource be reproduced or transmitted in any form or by any means, electronic or mechanical, including photocopying, recording, or any information storage or retrieval system without permission in writing from the copyright holder or that holder's agent.

3. Use of Alpha resources is permitted only when in conjunction with the running or promotion of an Alpha course. Resale, or the obtaining of payment in any other connection with any Alpha resource, is not permitted.

4. Alpha International asks that the name 'Alpha', or names similar to it, should not be used in connection with any other Christian course. This request is made to: avoid confusion caused by different courses having similar titles and is to ensure the uniformity and integrity of the Alpha course; and to maintain confidence in courses listed on the Alpha register.

5. Alpha International accepts that minor adaptations to the Alpha course may occasionally be desirable. These should only concern the length of the talks or the number of sessions. In each case the essential character of the course must be retained. Alpha is a series of about 15 talks, given over a period of time, including a weekend or day away, with teaching based on all the material in *Questions of Life*.

If the Alpha course is adapted the person responsible must: only use such a course in their own church or parish; not allow such a course to be used elsewhere; and not publish or promote such a course.

This statement supersedes all previous statements relating to copyright in any Alpha resource.